Based on the Common Core State Standards (CCSS)

PARCC

SUCCESS STRATEGIES

High School Geometry

Comprehensive Skill Building
Practice for the Partnership
for Assessment of Readiness
for College and Careers
Assessments

Dear Future Exam Success Story:

First of all, **THANK YOU** for purchasing Mometrix study materials!

Second, congratulations! You are one of the few determined test-takers who are committed to doing whatever it takes to excel on your exam. **You have come to the right place.** We developed these study materials with one goal in mind: to deliver you the information you need in a format that's concise and easy to use.

In addition to optimizing your guide for the content of the test, we've outlined our recommended steps for breaking down the preparation process into small, attainable goals so you can make sure you stay on track.

We've also analyzed the entire test-taking process, identifying the most common pitfalls and showing how you can overcome them and be ready for any curveball the test throws you.

Standardized testing is one of the biggest obstacles on your road to success, which only increases the importance of doing well in the high-pressure, high-stakes environment of test day. Your results on this test could have a significant impact on your future, and this guide provides the information and practical advice to help you achieve your full potential on test day.

Your success is our success

We would love to hear from you! If you would like to share the story of your exam success or if you have any questions or comments in regard to our products, please contact us at **800-673-8175** or **support@mometrix.com**.

Thanks again for your business and we wish you continued success!

Sincerely,
The Mometrix Test Preparation Team

Need more help? Check out our flashcards at: http://MometrixFlashcards.com/PARCC

TABLE OF CONTENTS

Introduction

Thank you for purchasing this resource! You have made the choice to prepare yourself for a test that could have a huge impact on your future, and this guide is designed to help you be fully ready for test day. Obviously, it's important to have a solid understanding of the test material, but you also need to be prepared for the unique environment and stressors of the test, so that you can perform to the best of your abilities.

For this purpose, the first section that appears in this guide is the **Success Strategies**. We've devoted countless hours to meticulously researching what works and what doesn't, and we've boiled down our findings to the five most impactful steps you can take to improve your performance on the test. We start at the beginning with study planning and move through the preparation process, all the way to the testing strategies that will help you get the most out of what you know when you're finally sitting in front of the test.

We recommend that you start preparing for your test as far in advance as possible. However, if you've bought this guide as a last-minute study resource and only have a few days before your test, we recommend that you skip over the first two Success Strategies since they address a long-term study plan.

If you struggle with **test anxiety**, we strongly encourage you to check out our recommendations for how you can overcome it. Test anxiety is a formidable foe, but it can be beaten, and we want to make sure you have the tools you need to defeat it.

Success Strategy #1 – Plan Big, Study Small

There's a lot riding on your performance. If you want to ace this test, you're going to need to keep your skills sharp and the material fresh in your mind. You need a plan that lets you review everything you need to know while still fitting in your schedule. We'll break this strategy down into three categories.

Information Organization

Start with the information you already have: the official test outline. From this, you can make a complete list of all the concepts you need to cover before the test. Organize these concepts into groups that can be studied together, and create a list of any related vocabulary you need to learn so you can brush up on any difficult terms. You'll want to keep this vocabulary list handy once you actually start studying since you may need to add to it along the way.

Time Management

Once you have your set of study concepts, decide how to spread them out over the time you have left before the test. Break your study plan into small, clear goals so you have a manageable task for each day and know exactly what you're doing. Then just focus on one small step at a time. When you manage your time this way, you don't need to spend hours at a time studying. Studying a small block of content for a short period each day helps you retain information better and avoid stressing over how much you have left to do. You can relax knowing that you have a plan to cover everything in time. In order for this strategy to be effective though, you have to start studying early and stick to your schedule. Avoid the exhaustion and futility that comes from last-minute cramming!

Study Environment

The environment you study in has a big impact on your learning. Studying in a coffee shop, while probably more enjoyable, is not likely to be as fruitful as studying in a quiet room. It's important to keep distractions to a minimum. You're only planning to study for a short block of time, so make the most of it. Don't pause to check your phone or get up to find a snack. It's also important to **avoid multitasking**. Research has consistently shown that multitasking will make your studying dramatically less effective. Your study area should also be comfortable and well-lit so you don't have the distraction of straining your eyes or sitting on an uncomfortable chair.

The time of day you study is also important. You want to be rested and alert. Don't wait until just before bedtime. Study when you'll be most likely to comprehend and remember. Even better, if you know what time of day your test will be, set that time aside for study. That way your brain will be used to working on that subject at that specific time and you'll have a better chance of recalling information.

Finally, it can be helpful to team up with others who are studying for the same test. Your actual studying should be done in as isolated an environment as possible, but the work of organizing the information and setting up the study plan can be divided up. In between study sessions, you can discuss with your teammates the concepts that you're all studying and quiz each other on the details. Just be sure that your teammates are as serious about the test as you are. If you find that your study time is being replaced with social time, you might need to find a new team.

Success Strategy #2 – Make Your Studying Count

You're devoting a lot of time and effort to preparing for this test, so you want to be absolutely certain it will pay off. This means doing more than just reading the content and hoping you can remember it on test day. It's important to make every minute of study count. There are two main areas you can focus on to make your studying count:

Retention

It doesn't matter how much time you study if you can't remember the material. You need to make sure you are retaining the concepts. To check your retention of the information you're learning, try recalling it at later times with minimal prompting. Try carrying around flashcards and glance at one or two from time to time or ask a friend who's also studying for the test to quiz you.

To enhance your retention, look for ways to put the information into practice so that you can apply it rather than simply recalling it. If you're using the information in practical ways, it will be much easier to remember. Similarly, it helps to solidify a concept in your mind if you're not only reading it to yourself but also explaining it to someone else. Ask a friend to let you teach them about a concept you're a little shaky on (or speak aloud to an imaginary audience if necessary). As you try to summarize, define, give examples, and answer your friend's questions, you'll understand the concepts better and they will stay with you longer. Finally, step back for a big picture view and ask yourself how each piece of information fits with the whole subject. When you link the different concepts together and see them working together as a whole, it's easier to remember the individual components.

Finally, practice showing your work on any multi-step problems, even if you're just studying. Writing out each step you take to solve a problem will help solidify the process in your mind, and you'll be more likely to remember it during the test.

Modality

Modality simply refers to the means or method by which you study. Choosing a study modality that fits your own individual learning style is crucial. No two people learn best in exactly the same way, so it's important to know your strengths and use them to your advantage.

For example, if you learn best by visualization, focus on visualizing a concept in your mind and draw an image or a diagram. Try color-coding your notes, illustrating them, or creating symbols that will trigger your mind to recall a learned concept. If you learn best by hearing or discussing information, find a study partner who learns the same way or read aloud to yourself. Think about how to put the information in your own words. Imagine that you are giving a lecture on the topic and record yourself so you can listen to it later.

For any learning style, flashcards can be helpful. Organize the information so you can take advantage of spare moments to review. Underline key words or phrases. Use different colors for different categories. Mnemonic devices (such as creating a short list in which every item starts with the same letter) can also help with retention. Find what works best for you and use it to store the information in your mind most effectively and easily.

Success Strategy #3 – Practice the Right Way

Your success on test day depends not only on how many hours you put into preparing, but also on whether you prepared the right way. It's good to check along the way to see if your studying is paying off. One of the most effective ways to do this is by taking practice tests to evaluate your progress. Practice tests are useful because they show exactly where you need to improve. Every time you take a practice test, pay special attention to these three groups of questions:

- The questions you got wrong
- The questions you had to guess on, even if you guessed right
- The questions you found difficult or slow to work through

This will show you exactly what your weak areas are, and where you need to devote more study time. Ask yourself why each of these questions gave you trouble. Was it because you didn't understand the material? Was it because you didn't remember the vocabulary? Do you need more repetitions on this type of question to build speed and confidence? Dig into those questions and figure out how you can strengthen your weak areas as you go back to review the material.

Additionally, many practice tests have a section explaining the answer choices. It can be tempting to read the explanation and think that you now have a good understanding of the concept. However, an explanation likely only covers part of the question's broader context. Even if the explanation makes sense, **go back and investigate** every concept related to the question until you're positive you have a thorough understanding.

As you go along, keep in mind that the practice test is just that: practice. Memorizing these questions and answers will not be very helpful on the actual test because it is unlikely to have any of the same exact questions. If you only know the right answers to the sample questions, you won't be prepared for the real thing. **Study the concepts** until you understand them fully, and then you'll be able to answer any question that shows up on the test.

It's important to wait on the practice tests until you're ready. If you take a test on your first day of study, you may be overwhelmed by the amount of material covered and how much you need to learn. Work up to it gradually.

On test day, you'll need to be prepared for answering questions, managing your time, and using the test-taking strategies you've learned. It's a lot to balance, like a mental marathon that will have a big impact on your future. Like training for a marathon, you'll need to start slowly and work your way up. When test day arrives, you'll be ready.

Start with what you've read in the first two Success Strategies—plan your course and study in the way that works best for you. If you have time, consider using multiple study resources to get different approaches to the same concepts. It can be helpful to see difficult concepts from more than one angle. Then find a good source for practice tests. Many times, the test website will suggest potential study resources or provide sample tests.

Practice Test Strategy

If you're able to find at least three practice tests, we recommend this strategy:

Untimed and Open-Book Practice

Take the first test with no time constraints and with your notes and study guide handy. Take your time and focus on applying the strategies you've learned.

Timed and Open-Book Practice

Take the second practice test open-book as well, but set a timer and practice pacing yourself to finish in time.

Timed and Closed-Book Practice

Take any other practice tests as if it were test day. Set a timer and put away your study materials. Sit at a table or desk in a quiet room, imagine yourself at the testing center, and answer questions as quickly and accurately as possible.

Keep repeating timed and closed-book tests on a regular basis until you run out of practice tests or it's time for the actual test. Your mind will be ready for the schedule and stress of test day, and you'll be able to focus on recalling the material you've learned.

- 5 -

Success Strategy #4 – Pace Yourself

Once you're fully prepared for the material on the test, your biggest challenge on test day will be managing your time. Just knowing that the clock is ticking can make you panic even if you have plenty of time left. Work on pacing yourself so you can build confidence against the time constraints of the exam. Pacing is a difficult skill to master, especially in a high-pressure environment, so **practice is vital.**

Set time expectations for your pace based on how much time is available. For example, if a section has 60 questions and the time limit is 30 minutes, you know you have to average 30 seconds or less per question in order to answer them all. Although 30 seconds is the hard limit, set 25 seconds per question as your goal, so you reserve extra time to spend on harder questions. When you budget extra time for the harder questions, you no longer have any reason to stress when those questions take longer to answer.

Don't let this time expectation distract you from working through the test at a calm, steady pace, but keep it in mind so you don't spend too much time on any one question. Recognize that taking extra time on one question you don't understand may keep you from answering two that you do understand later in the test. If your time limit for a question is up and you're still not sure of the answer, mark it and move on, and come back to it later if the time and the test format allow. If the testing format doesn't allow you to return to earlier questions, just make an educated guess; then put it out of your mind and move on.

On the easier questions, be careful not to rush. It may seem wise to hurry through them so you have more time for the challenging ones, but it's not worth missing one if you know the concept and just didn't take the time to read the question fully. Work efficiently but make sure you understand the question and have looked at all of the answer choices, since more than one may seem right at first.

Even if you're paying attention to the time, you may find yourself a little behind at some point. You should speed up to get back on track, but do so wisely. Don't panic; just take a few seconds less on each question until you're caught up. Don't guess without thinking, but do look through the answer choices and eliminate any you know are wrong. If you can get down to two choices, it is often worthwhile to guess from those. Once you've chosen an answer, move on and don't dwell on any that you skipped or had to hurry through. If a question was taking too long, chances are it was one of the harder ones, so you weren't as likely to get it right anyway.

On the other hand, if you find yourself getting ahead of schedule, it may be beneficial to slow down a little. The more quickly you work, the more likely you are to make a careless mistake that will affect your score. You've budgeted time for each question, so don't be afraid to spend that time. Practice an efficient but careful pace to get the most out of the time you have.

- 6 -

Test-Taking Strategies

This section contains a list of test-taking strategies that you may find helpful as you work through the test. By taking what you know and applying logical thought, you can maximize your chances of answering any question correctly!

It is very important to realize that every question is different and every person is different: no single strategy will work on every question, and no single strategy will work for every person. That's why we've included all of them here, so you can try them out and determine which ones work best for different types of questions and which ones work best for you.

Question Strategies

Read Carefully

Read the question and answer choices carefully. Don't miss the question because you misread the terms. You have plenty of time to read each question thoroughly and make sure you understand what is being asked. Yet a happy medium must be attained, so don't waste too much time. You must read carefully, but efficiently.

Contextual Clues

Look for contextual clues. If the question includes a word you are not familiar with, look at the immediate context for some indication of what the word might mean. Contextual clues can often give you all the information you need to decipher the meaning of an unfamiliar word. Even if you can't determine the meaning, you may be able to narrow down the possibilities enough to make a solid guess at the answer to the question.

Prefixes

If you're having trouble with a word in the question or answer choices, try dissecting it. Take advantage of every clue that the word might include. Prefixes and suffixes can be a huge help. Usually they allow you to determine a basic meaning. Pre- means before, post- means after, pro - is positive, de- is negative. From prefixes and suffixes, you can get an idea of the general meaning of the word and try to put it into context.

Hedge Words

Watch out for critical hedge words, such as *likely, may, can, sometimes, often, almost, mostly, usually, generally, rarely,* and *sometimes*. Question writers insert these hedge phrases to cover every possibility. Often an answer choice will be wrong simply because it leaves no room for exception. Be on guard for answer choices that have definitive words such as *exactly* and *always*.

Switchback Words

Stay alert for *switchbacks*. These are the words and phrases frequently used to alert you to shifts in thought. The most common switchback words are *but, although,* and *however*. Others include *nevertheless, on the other hand, even though, while, in spite of, despite, regardless of*. Switchback words are important to catch because they can change the direction of the question or an answer choice.

Face Value

When in doubt, use common sense. Accept the situation in the problem at face value. Don't read too much into it. These problems will not require you to make wild assumptions. If you have to go beyond creativity and warp time or space in order to have an answer choice fit the question, then you should move on and consider the other answer choices. These are normal problems rooted in reality. The applicable relationship or explanation may not be readily apparent, but it is there for you to figure out. Use your common sense to interpret anything that isn't clear

Answer Choice Strategies

Answer Selection

The most thorough way to pick an answer choice is to identify and eliminate wrong answers until only one is left, then confirm it is the correct answer. Sometimes an answer choice may immediately seem right, but be careful. The test writers will usually put more than one reasonable answer choice on each question, so take a second to read all of them and make sure that the other choices are not equally obvious. As long as you have time left, it is better to read every answer choice than to pick the first one that looks right without checking the others.

Answer Choice Families

An answer choice family consists of two (in rare cases, three) answer choices that are very similar in construction and cannot all be true at the same time. If you see two answer choices that are direct opposites or parallels, one of them is usually the correct answer. For instance, if one answer choice says that quantity x increases and another either says that quantity x decreases (opposite) or says that quantity y increases (parallel), then those answer choices would fall into the same family. An answer choice that doesn't match the construction of the answer choice family is more likely to be incorrect. Most questions will not have answer choice families, but when they do appear, you should be prepared to recognize them.

Eliminate Answers

Eliminate answer choices as soon as you realize they are wrong, but make sure you consider all possibilities. If you are eliminating answer choices and realize that the last one you are left with is also wrong, don't panic. Start over and consider each choice again. There may be something you missed the first time that you will realize on the second pass.

Avoid Fact Traps

Don't be distracted by an answer choice that is factually true but doesn't answer the question. You are looking for the choice that answers the question. Stay focused on what the question is asking for so you don't accidentally pick an answer that is true but incorrect. Always go back to the question and make sure the answer choice you've selected actually answers the question and is not merely a true statement.

Extreme Statements

In general, you should avoid answers that put forth extreme actions as standard practice or proclaim controversial ideas as established fact. An answer choice that states the "process should be used in certain situations, if..." is much more likely to be correct than one that states the "process should be discontinued completely." The first is a calm rational statement and doesn't even make a definitive, uncompromising stance, using a hedge word *if* to provide wiggle room, whereas the second choice is a radical idea and far more extreme.

Benchmark

As you read through the answer choices and you come across one that seems to answer the question well, mentally select that answer choice. This is not your final answer, but it's the one that will help you evaluate the other answer choices. The one that you selected is your benchmark or standard for judging each of the other answer choices. Every other answer choice must be compared to your benchmark. That choice is correct until proven otherwise by another answer choice beating it. If you find a better answer, then that one becomes your new benchmark. Once you've decided that no other choice answers the question as well as your benchmark, you have your final answer.

Predict the Answer

Before you even start looking at the answer choices, it is often best to try to predict the answer. When you come up with the answer on your own, it is easier to avoid distractions and traps because you will know exactly what to look for. The right answer choice is unlikely to be word-for-word what you came up with, but it should be a close match. Even if you are confident that you have the right answer, you should still take the time to read each option before moving on.

General Strategies

Tough Questions

If you are stumped on a problem or it appears too hard or too difficult, don't waste time. Move on! Remember though, if you can quickly check for obviously incorrect answer choices, your chances of guessing correctly are greatly improved. Before you completely give up, at least try to knock out a couple of possible answers. Eliminate what you can and then guess at the remaining answer choices before moving on.

Check Your Work

Since you will probably not know every term listed and the answer to every question, it is important that you get credit for the ones that you do know. Don't miss any questions through careless mistakes. If at all possible, try to take a second to look back over your answer selection and make sure you've selected the correct answer choice and haven't made a costly careless mistake (such as marking an answer choice that you didn't mean to mark). This quick double check should more than pay for itself in caught mistakes for the time it costs.

Pace Yourself

It's easy to be overwhelmed when you're looking at a page full of questions; your mind is confused and full of random thoughts, and the clock is ticking down faster than you would like. Calm down and maintain the pace that you have set for yourself. Especially as you get down to the last few minutes of the test, don't let the small numbers on the clock make you panic. As long as you are on track by monitoring your pace, you are guaranteed to have time for each question.

Don't Rush

It is very easy to make errors when you are in a hurry. Maintaining a fast pace in answering questions is pointless if it makes you miss questions that you would have gotten right otherwise. Test writers like to include distracting information and wrong answers that seem right. Taking a little extra time to avoid careless mistakes can make all the difference in your test score. Find a pace that allows you to be confident in the answers that you select.

Keep Moving

Panicking will not help you pass the test, so do your best to stay calm and keep moving. Taking deep breaths and going through the answer elimination steps you practiced can help to break through a stress barrier and keep your pace.

Final Notes

The combination of a solid foundation of content knowledge and the confidence that comes from practicing your plan for applying that knowledge is the key to maximizing your performance on test day. As your foundation of content knowledge is built up and strengthened, you'll find that the strategies included in this chapter become more and more effective in helping you quickly sift through the distractions and traps of the test to isolate the correct answer.

Now it's time to move on to the test content chapters of this book, but be sure to keep your goal in mind. As you read, think about how you will be able to apply this information on the test. If you've already seen sample questions for the test and you have an idea of the question format and style, try to come up with questions of your own that you can answer based on what you're reading. This will give you valuable practice applying your knowledge in the same ways you can expect to on test day.

Good luck and good studying!

Congruence

Point and line

A point is a specific location and is used to help understand and define all other concepts in geometry. A point is denoted by a single capital letter, such as point P.

A line is a straight continuous set of points and usually denoted by two points in that set. For instance, $\overleftrightarrow{AB}$ is the line which passes through points A and B.

The distance along a line, or the distance between two points on a line, can be measured using a ruler. If the two points are located on the Cartesian plane, the distance can be found using the distance formula: $d = \sqrt{(x_2 - x_1)^2 + (y_2 - y_1)^2}$.

The distance around a circular arc, or the distance along a circle between two points, can be measured using a piece of string (to follow the shape of the circle) and then a ruler. The distance can also be found by finding the portion of the circle's circumference represented by the arc.

Angle, circle, perpendicular lines, parallel lines and line segment

Angle – The set of points which are part of two lines that intersect at a specific point. An angle is made up of two "half lines" called rays that begin at the shared point, called the vertex, and extend away from that point. An angle can be denoted simply by the angle's vertex ($\angle A$ or $\sphericalangle A$) or by three points: one from one ray, the point of intersection, and one from the second ray ($\angle BAC$ or $\sphericalangle BAC$).

Circle – A continuous set of points which are all equidistant from a separate point called the center. A circle usually shares the same label as its center: circle P with center at point P.

Perpendicular lines – Two lines which intersect at one specific point and create four 90° angles. Notation: $\overleftrightarrow{DE} \perp \overleftrightarrow{EF}$ when lines DE and EF intersect and form right angles at point E.

Parallel lines – Two lines which do not share any points and never intersect. Notation: $\overleftrightarrow{GH} \parallel \overleftrightarrow{IJ}$.

Line segment – The section of a line that is between two specific points on that line, usually denoted by two points: $\overline{KL}$.

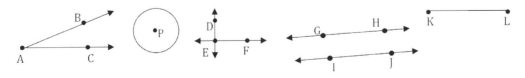

Rotation, center of rotation, and angle of rotation

A rotation is a transformation that turns a figure around a point called the center of rotation, which can lie anywhere in the plane. If a line is drawn from a point on a figure to the center of rotation, and another line is drawn from the center to the rotated image of that point, the angle between the two lines is the angle of rotation. The vertex of the angle of rotation is the center of rotation.

Reflection over a line and reflection in a point

A reflection of a figure over a line (a "flip") creates a congruent image that is the same distance from the line as the original figure but on the opposite side. The line of reflection is the perpendicular bisector of any line segment drawn from a point on the original figure to its reflected image (unless the point and its reflected image happen to be the same point, which happens when a figure is reflected over one of its own sides).

A reflection of a figure in a point is the same as the rotation of the figure 180° about that point. The image of the figure is congruent to the original figure. The point of reflection is the midpoint of a line segment which connects a point in the figure to its image (unless the point and its reflected image happen to be the same point, which happens when a figure is reflected in one of its own points).

Translation

A translation is a transformation which slides a figure from one position in the plane to another position in the plane. The original figure and the translated figure have the same size, shape, and orientation.

Transforming a given figure using rotation, reflection, and translation

To rotate a given figure: 1. Identify the point of rotation. 2. Using tracing paper, geometry software, or by approximation, recreate the figure at a new location around the point of rotation.

To reflect a given figure: 1. Identify the line of reflection. 2. By folding the paper, using geometry software, or by approximation, recreate the image at a new location on the other side of the line of reflection.

To translate a given figure: 1. Identify the new location. 2. Using graph paper, geometry software, or by approximation, recreate the figure in the new location. If using graph paper, make a chart of the x- and y-values to keep track of the coordinates of all critical points.

Identifying what transformation was used when given a figure and its transformed image

To identify that a figure has been rotated, look for evidence that the figure is still face-up, but has changed its orientation.

To identify that a figure has been reflected across a line, look for evidence that the figure is now face-down.

To identify that a figure has been translated, look for evidence that a figure is still face-up and has not changed orientation; the only change is location.

To identify that a figure has been dilated, look for evidence that the figure has changed its size but not its orientation.

Dilation

A dilation is a transformation which proportionally stretches or shrinks a figure by a scale factor. The dilated image is the same shape and orientation as the original image but a different size. A polygon and its dilated image are similar.

Using transparencies to represent transformations

After drawing a shape on a piece of transparency, the shape can be rotated by leaving the transparency on a flat surface and turning it clockwise or counterclockwise.

After drawing a shape on a piece of transparency, the shape can be translated by leaving the transparency on a flat surface and sliding it in any direction (left, right, up, down, or along a diagonal).

After drawing a shape on a piece of transparency, the shape can be reflected by turning the transparency over so that the side the shape is on the underside of the transparency, touching the table.

Using functions to represent a translation on the Cartesian plane

First, determine the points which define the shape. Second, use an equation or equations to express how the vertices of the shape are moving. When the shape is translated both vertically and horizontally, the translation can be expressed using two equations: one for the x-values and one for the y-values.

For example, consider a triangle, which is defined by its vertices at three specific ordered pairs. Adding 5 to each of the x-values will create a second triangle five units to the right of the first triangle; the equation representing this transformation is $x_2 = x_1 + 5$, where x_1 represents the x-coordinates of the original triangle and x_2 represents the x-coordinates of the translated triangle. If the triangle is also moved four units downward, the equation $y_2 = y_1 - 4$ can be used to find the new y=coordinates, represented by y_2, from the triangle's original y-coordinates, represented by y_1. Together, the horizontal and vertical shift can be written as $\begin{cases} x_2 = x_1 + 5 \\ y_2 = y_1 - 4 \end{cases}$, and these equations would be used to transform each vertex like so:

first point (x_1, y_1)	first vertex (3,6)	second vertex (5,1)	third vertex (4, −1)
x-values: $x_2 = x_1 + 5$	$x_2 = 3 + 5 = 8$	$x_2 = 5 + 5 = 10$	$x_2 = 4 + 5 = 9$
y-values: $y_2 = y_1 - 4$	$y_2 = 6 - 4 = 2$	$y_2 = 1 - 4 = -3$	$y_2 = -1 - 4 = -5$
new point (x_2, y_2)	first vertex (8,2)	second vertex (10,−3)	third vertex (9,−5)

A triangle with vertices (3,6), (5,1), and (4,-1) shifted five units to the right and four units down results in a triangle with vertices (8,2), (10,-3), and (9,-5).

- 14 -

Translated vs. stretched horizontally shapes

When a figure is translated, it moves to another location within the plane; since each point is shifted by the same distance, its size and shape remain the same. When a figure is stretched horizontally, its size and shape are affected. For example, consider an equilateral triangle which has a horizontal base. If the two endpoints of the base are pulled horizontally in opposite directions, the angle opposite the base widens as the two other angles become smaller. So, the lengths of the sides and the angle measures change, and the resulting triangle differs in both size and shape from the original triangle.

Rotations and reflections which carry a rectangle onto itself

A rectangle will be carried onto itself when it is rotated any multiple of 180° either clockwise or counterclockwise about its center. If the rectangle is a square, a rotation of 90° or any multiple of 90° clockwise or counterclockwise about the center will carry the square onto itself.

Any rectangle will be carried onto itself when it is rotated 360° or any multiple of 360° about any point either clockwise or counterclockwise

A rectangle will also be carried onto itself when it is reflected over any of its lines of symmetry. A rectangle has two lines of symmetry, and a square has four.

Using transformations (rotations and reflections) to carry a parallelogram onto itself.

A parallelogram will be carried onto itself when it is rotated by any multiple of 180° either clockwise or counterclockwise about its center. A square or any other rhombus is carried onto itself when it is rotated about its center by a multiple of 90°.

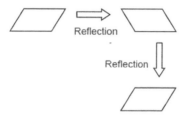

Any parallelogram will be carried onto itself when it is rotated 360° or any multiple of 360° about any point either clockwise or counterclockwise.

A square or other rhombus reflected across any of its four lines of symmetry will map onto itself, and a rectangle reflected across either of its two line of symmetry will be carried onto itself. Other parallelograms have no lines of symmetry and can therefore not be reflected onto themselves.

Rotations and reflections which carry a trapezoid onto itself

A trapezoid will be carried onto itself when it is rotated 360° or any multiple of 360° either clockwise or counterclockwise.

A trapezoid will be carried onto itself when it is reflected over its line of symmetry, which is the perpendicular bisector of its two parallel sides.

Rotations and reflections which carry a regular polygon onto itself

A regular polygon will be carried onto itself when it is rotated about its center either clockwise or counterclockwise by 360°/n, where n is the number of sides of the polygon.

Any polygon will be carried onto itself when it is rotated 360° or any multiple of 360° about any point either clockwise or counterclockwise.

A regular polygon will be carried onto itself when it is reflected over any of its lines of symmetry.

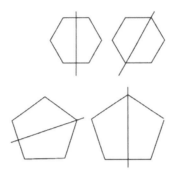

Congruence of two figures in terms of rigid motion

Two figures are congruent if one figure can be made to carry onto the second figure using one or more rotations, reflections, and/or translations.

Two triangles are congruent in terms of rigid motion when one triangle is the image of the other triangle. In one triangle, each side and angle is matched with only one side or angle of the other triangle. If a series of rigid motions align the two triangles, then the sides that are the same and the angles that are the same will be matched. If the sides and angles are all matched, then the congruent triangles have six congruent parts. Thus, the parts that correspond after transformation are congruent with each other.

Use the definition of congruence in terms of rigid motion to describe the criteria for angle-side-angle (ASA) congruence for triangles

A figure is congruent to another figure if one can be superimposed on the other by rigid motion (translation, reflection, rotation). When two congruent triangles are superimposed, it two angles and the side between the two angles align, the other two sides and angle will also align, Therefore, it is sufficient to show when proving two triangles congruent that two angles and the side between the angles are the same.

- 16 -

Use the definition of congruence in terms of rigid motion to describe the criteria for side-angle-side (SAS) congruence for triangles

 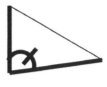

A figure is congruent to another figure if one can be superimposed on the other by rigid motion (translation, reflection, rotation). When two congruent triangles are superimposed, it two sides and the angle between the two angles align, the other side and two angles will also align, Therefore, it is sufficient to show when proving two triangles congruent that two sides and the angle between the sides are the same.

Use the definition of congruence in terms of rigid motion to describe the criteria for side-side-side (SSS) congruence for triangles

A figure is congruent to another figure if one can be superimposed on the other by rigid motion (translation, reflection, rotation). When two congruent triangles are superimposed, if all three sides align, the three angles will also align, therefore, it is sufficient to show when proving two triangles congruent that the measures of the three sides of the one triangle are equal to the measures of the three sides of the other.

Show that vertical angles are congruent

Draw two lines which intersect at a point. This point of intersection becomes a shared vertex of four angles created by the intersection of the two lines. Vertical angles are across from each other, and there are two pairs of vertical angles formed by the intersection of two lines. When one angle is rotated about the point of intersection by 180°, it aligns with its vertical angle. Therefore, the two angles are congruent.

- 17 -

Show that when two parallel lines are cut by a transversal, the resulting alternate interior angles are congruent. Showing that when two parallel lines are cut by a transversal, the resulting corresponding angles are congruent

Draw two parallel lines cut by a transversal and note two alternate interior angles. Using the midpoint of the transversal segment between the two parallel lines as a point of rotation, rotate half of the figure onto the other half of the figure. The two noted angles align and are therefore congruent.

Draw two parallel lines cut by a transversal and note two corresponding angles. Translate one parallel line along the transversal until it aligns with the other parallel line. The two noted angles align and are therefore congruent.

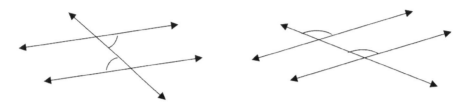

Show the measures of the interior angles of a triangle add to $180°$

Draw a line on a piece of paper. Cut each of the sides of the triangle at the midpoint to create three angles. Transform the three angles using rotation to align all three so their vertices are at the same point. Two of the angles' sides are parallel to the line, and the third angle's sides touch the other sides of the angles. Because the three angles come together to form a line, which measures $180°$, the three angles add to $180°$.

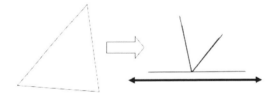

Base angles of an isosceles triangle are congruent

Draw an isosceles triangle. Reflect one side of the triangle across the perpendicular bisector of the base. The two base angles align and are therefore congruent.

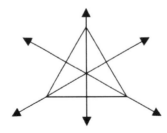

Three medians of a triangle meet at a point

Draw a triangle. From each vertex, draw a line to the midpoint of the opposite side. These three medians intersect at one point in the triangle. Show that this is true for acute, right, and obtuse triangles.

Show that the segment which joins the midpoints of two sides of a triangle is parallel to the third side and half its length.

Draw a triangle and construct a line segment which connects the midpoints of two sides of the triangle. Translate the line segment so that it aligns with the third side and one endpoint of the segment is aligned with the endpoint of the third side. Since the line segment was able to be translated without rotation, it is parallel to the third side of the triangle.

Draw a line that is perpendicular to the third side of the triangle through the translated segment's endpoint which does not lie on the triangle's vertex. Reflect the line segment across this line. The endpoint that was aligned with the first vertex is now aligned with the second vertex; thus, the line segment is half the length of the third side of the triangle.

Opposite sides of parallelograms are congruent

Draw a parallelogram. Translate one side of the parallelogram along the adjacent sides until it is aligned with the opposite side. The endpoints align, so the sides are congruent.

Opposite angles of parallelograms are congruent

Use the point where the diagonals intersect as a point of rotation. Rotate the parallelogram 180° so that the angles are aligned with the angles opposite them.

Diagonals of parallelograms bisect each other

Draw a parallelogram and its two diagonals. Use one diagonal as a line of reflection. Reflect the other diagonal onto itself. Since the endpoints align, the line of reflection is a bisector of the reflected diagonal. Repeat the process for the other diagonal.

A rectangle is a parallelogram with congruent diagonals

A rectangle is a parallelogram with four right angles. Draw a rectangle and its two diagonals. Find the midpoints of two opposite sides of the rectangle and connect them to construct a line of reflection. Reflect one of the right triangles over the line of reflection. The reflected triangle's hypotenuse, which is the one of the rectangle's diagonals, aligns with another triangle's hypotenuse, which is the rectangle's other diagonal. Thus, the diagonals are congruent, so a rectangle is a parallelogram with congruent diagonals.

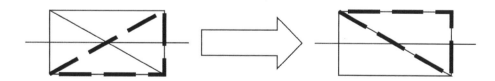

- 19 -

Tools used in geometric constructions

- Compass – A tool used to draw circles and to measure distances from a single point. A compass is used for translations and copying figures.
- Straightedge – A tool used to draw straight lines and line segments and to measure distances between two points. A straightedge is used to keep lines neat and straight when constructing or copying figures.
- Protractor – A tool used to measure angles. A protractor is used for rotations and constructions of polygons.
- String – A tool used to measure distances either from a single point or between two points. String is used in rotations and to copy figures.
- Reflective devices – A variety of tools used to reflect an image.
- Paper folding – A technique used to reflect images onto figures or portions of figures onto themselves. Paper folding is used in reflections and constructions.

Geometry software also exists to construct and copy figures on the computer.

Compass

Using a compass to construct a copy of a segment

Use a compass to measure the length of the segment by placing the stationary end on one endpoint and opening the compass so the pencil end is on the other endpoint. Draw a point elsewhere and place the compass tip on the point, then draw an arc with the pencil. Any line segment drawn from the initial point to any point on the arc will be a copy of the first segment.

Compass and a straightedge

Using a compass and a straightedge to construct a copy of an angle

Place the stationary end of a compass at the vertex of the angle and construct an arc that intersects both rays. Use a straightedge to construct a ray elsewhere, and without changing the compass opening, draw an arc by positioning the compass at its endpoint. Then, on the original angle, place the compass tip on the point where the arc intersects one of the rays and adjust the compass so that the pencil meets the point where the arc intersects the other ray; draw a small arc that passes through this point. Without changing the compass opening, place the compass tip on the intersection of the ray and the arc and draw a second arc which intersects the first. From the ray's endpoint, draw using a straightedge another ray through the intersection of the two arcs on the construction. This angle is a copy of the first angle.

Using a compass and a straightedge to construct an angle bisector

Place the compass tip on the vertex of the angle. Draw an arc that intersects both rays of the angle. Move the compass tip to one of the intersections. Draw a small arc inside the angle, beyond the first arc, making the compass opening smaller if necessary. Without changing the compass opening, move the compass tip to the other ray at the point at which it intersects the first arc. Draw another small arc inside the angle that intersects the last arc. Use a straightedge to draw a line through the vertex of the angle and the intersection of the two small arcs. This line is the angle bisector.

Using a compass and a straightedge to construct perpendicular lines

Draw two points and use a straightedge to draw a line through the points. Place the compass tip on one of the points and draw two arcs, one above the line and one below the line. Without changing the compass opening, from the other point, draw two more arcs that intersect the first two. Construct a line through these two intersections. This line is perpendicular to the first line.

Using a compass and a straightedge to construct a line segment and its perpendicular bisector

Using a straightedge, draw a line segment. Open the width of the compass so that it is greater than half the width of the line segment. Place the compass tip on one of the endpoints and draw two arcs, one above and one below the line segment. Without changing the compass opening, from the other endpoint, draw two more arcs that intersect the first two. Using a straightedge, construct a line through these two intersections. This line is a perpendicular bisector of the line segment.

Using a compass and straightedge to construct a line parallel to a given line through a point not on the line

Start with a line and a point not on the line. Use a straightedge to draw a ray from a point on the given line through the given point. With the compass tip at the intersection of the given line and the ray, construct an arc that intersects both. Without changing the compass opening, reposition the compass tip on the given point and draw a second arc similar to the first. Then, use the first arc to set the compass with such that one part of the compass touches point where the arc crosses the ray and the point where that arc crosses the original line. Without changing the compass opening, reposition the compass again to the given point and draw an arc through the second arc. Use the straightedge to draw a line which passes through the point of intersection of the second and third arcs and the given point. This line is parallel to the given line.

Using a compass and a straightedge to inscribe an equilateral triangle inside of a circle with a given center

Draw a point on the circle. Position the tip of a compass at the center of the circle and the pencil at this point so that the width of the compass is the circle's radius. Without changing the compass width, position the compass tip at the point on the circle and use a pencil to make an arc on the circle. Move the compass tip to the point at which this arc intersects the circle and make another arc on the circle. Continue this process all the way around the circle so that its circumference is equally divided into six pieces. Connect every other point using a straight edge to inscribe an equilateral triangle inside of the circle.

Using a compass and a straightedge to inscribe a square inside of a circle with a given center

Draw a diameter of the circle. Open the width of a compass so that it is greater than half the circle's radius. Place the compass tip at one of the endpoints of the diameter and draw an arc. Reposition the tip at the other endpoint and draw a second arc which intersects the first. Position a straightedge through this point of intersection and the center of the circle and draw a second diameter, which is the perpendicular bisector of the first. The endpoints of each of the two diameters are the vertices of a square. Connect the four vertices with a straight line to create a square inscribed in a circle.

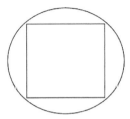

Using a compass and a straight edge to inscribe a regular hexagon inside of a circle with a given center

Draw a point on the circle. Position the tip of a compass at the center of the circle and the pencil at this point so that the width of the compass is the circle's radius. Without changing the compass width, position the compass tip at the point on the circle and use a pencil to make an arc on the circle. Move the compass tip to the point at which this arc intersects the circle and make another arc on the circle. Continue this process all the way around the circle so that its circumference is equally divided into six pieces. Connect each of these points using a straight edge to construct a regular hexagon inside of the circle.

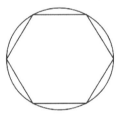

Paper folding

Using paper folding to construct a segment bisector

Fold the paper so that the endpoints of the line segment align. The point where the fold intersects the line segment is the midpoint. Any line, line segment, or ray drawn through this point is a segment bisector.

Using paper folding to construct a line parallel to a given line through a point not on the line

Start with a line and a point not on that line, both drawn on a sheet of paper. Fold the paper so that the fold passes through the point and so that the line is reflected onto itself over the fold. Unfold the paper and fold again, again so that the fold passes through the point not on the line, but so that the first fold is reflected onto itself. Unfold the paper and use a straightedge to draw a line along the second fold. This line is parallel to the first line and passes through the point not on the line.

Similarity, Right Triangles, and Trigonometry

Verifying that a dilation takes a line not passing through the center of the dilation to a parallel line, and leaves a line passing through the center unchanged

$\overleftrightarrow{AB}$ is a line that does not pass through the center of the dilation. When line segment $\overline{AB}$ is dilated using a scale factor of 2, line segment $\overline{A'B'}$ is created. Translate the intersection of $\overleftrightarrow{AB}$ and the line through A and the center of dilation to the intersection of $\overleftrightarrow{A'B'}$ and the line through A and the center of dilation. Since $\overleftrightarrow{AB}$ overlaps $\overleftrightarrow{A'B'}$, the two lines are parallel.

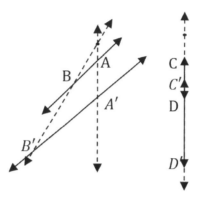

$\overleftrightarrow{CD}$ is a line that passes through the center of the dilation. When line segment $\overline{CD}$ is dilated using a scale factor of 2, $\overline{C'D'}$ is created. Both lines $\overleftrightarrow{CD}$ and $\overleftrightarrow{C'D'}$ are the same line which passes through the center of dilation, so the dilation left the line unchanged.

Verifying that a dilation of a line segment is longer or shorter than the original line segment in the ratio given by the scale factor

$\overline{AB}$ is a line segment that is dilated using a scale factor of ½. Translate $\overline{AB}$ along one line through the center of dilation until A is aligned with A'. Since the ratio is less than 1, $\overline{AB}$ is larger than $\overline{A'B'}$, so using the perpendicular bisector of $\overline{AB}$ as a line of reflection, reflect $\overline{A'B'}$ so that A' is now aligned with B. Since B' did not move, and is still at the point of intersection between $\overline{AB}$ and the perpendicular bisector, the ratio of $\overline{A'B'}$ to $\overline{AB}$ is 1 to 2.

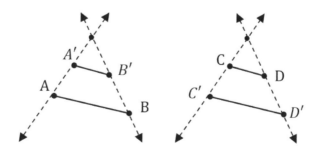

$\overline{CD}$ is a line segment that is dilated using a scale factor of 2. Translate $\overline{CD}$ along one line through the center of dilation until C is aligned with C'. Since the ratio is greater than 1, $\overline{C'D'}$ is larger than $\overline{CD}$, so using the perpendicular bisector of $\overline{C'D'}$ as a line of reflection, reflect $\overline{CD}$ so that C is now aligned

- 23 -

with D'. Since D did not move, and is still at the point of intersection between $\overline{C'D'}$ and the perpendicular bisector, the ratio of $\overline{C'D'}$ to $\overline{CD}$ is 2 to 1.

Using transformations and the definition of similarity to prove that two figures are similar

The corresponding angles of similar figures are congruent, and the corresponding sides are proportional. Rotate and translate one figure onto the other so that one pair of corresponding angles aligns. Continue to translate the figure so that corresponding angles are aligned, one pair of angles at a time. After verifying that all pairs of corresponding angles are congruent, determine if the sides are proportional. Position the figures so that corresponding sides are parallel and so that the smaller figure does not overlap the larger figure. Use a straightedge to draw lines that will connect each pair of corresponding vertices. Extend the lines to find a point of possible intersection. If all the lines meet at a single point, that point is the center of dilation and the two figures are similar.

Using transformations and the definition of similarity to show two triangles are similar if all corresponding pairs of angles are congruent and all corresponding pairs of sides are proportional

Rotate and translate one triangle so that one pair of corresponding angles aligns. Continue to translate the triangle so that corresponding angles are aligned, one pair of angles at a time. After verifying that all pairs of corresponding angles are congruent, determine if the sides are proportional. Position the triangles so that corresponding sides are parallel and so that the smaller triangle does not overlap the larger. Use a straightedge to draw lines that will connect each pair of corresponding vertices. Extend the lines to find a point of possible intersection. If all the lines meet at a single point, that point is the center of dilation and the two figures are similar.

Using the properties of similarity transformations to describe the criteria for angle-angle (AA) similarity of triangles

When a triangle is dilated (a similarity transformation) the lengths of its side change, but its angle measures remain the same. When an angle of a triangle is aligned with the corresponding angle of a dilated triangle, the two angles match; the same is true for the other two pairs of corresponding angles. When the corresponding angles of two triangles are congruent, the two triangles are similar. It is sufficient, however, to show that two of the three pairs of corresponding angles are congruent to determine the triangles' similarity: the third pair of corresponding angles must also be congruent since the sum of the angles in each triangle is $180°$.

Proving that a line which passes through a triangle and which is parallel to one of its sides divides the other two sides proportionally

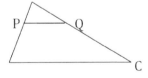

In the diagram, PQ is parallel to BC. When two parallel lines are cut by a transversal, corresponding angles are congruent. So, $\angle APQ \cong \angle PBC$ and, $\angle AQP \cong \angle QCB$. Thus, by the AA similarity theorem, $\triangle ABC$ is similar to $\triangle APQ$. The ratios of corresponding sides of similar triangles are proportional, so $\frac{AB}{AP} = \frac{AC}{AQ}$. Since $AB = AP + PB$ and $AC = AQ + QC$, $\frac{AP+PB}{AP} = \frac{AQ+QC}{AQ}$. This can be rewritten as $\frac{AP}{AP} +$

- 24 -

$\frac{PB}{AP} = \frac{AQ}{AQ} + \frac{QC}{AQ} \rightarrow 1 + \frac{PB}{AP} = 1 + \frac{QC}{AQ} \rightarrow \frac{PB}{AP} = \frac{QC}{AQ}$. Therefore, a line which passes through a triangle and which is parallel to one of its sides divides the other two sides proportionally.

Proving a line that divides two sides of a triangle proportionally is parallel to the third side

If line PQ divides $\triangle ABC$ proportionally, then $\frac{PB}{AP} = \frac{QC}{AQ}$.

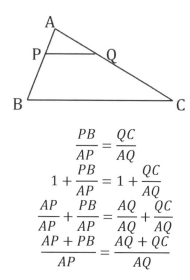

$$\frac{PB}{AP} = \frac{QC}{AQ}$$
$$1 + \frac{PB}{AP} = 1 + \frac{QC}{AQ}$$
$$\frac{AP}{AP} + \frac{PB}{AP} = \frac{AQ}{AQ} + \frac{QC}{AQ}$$
$$\frac{AP + PB}{AP} = \frac{AQ + QC}{AQ}$$

Since $AB = AP + PB$ and $AC = AQ + QC$, $\frac{AB}{AP} = \frac{AC}{AQ}$. Since $\angle BAC$ is shared with $\triangle ABC$ and $\triangle APQ$, and since the two sides flanking the angle are proportional, by SAS similarity, $\triangle ABC$ is similar to $\triangle APQ$. Corresponding angles of similar triangles are congruent, so $\angle APQ \cong \angle PBC$ and , $\angle AQP \cong \angle QCB$. When two lines, such as PQ and BC, are cut by a transversal, such as AB, and corresponding angles, such as so $\angle APQ$ and $\angle PBC$ are congruent, the two lines are parallel. So, PQ is parallel to BC. Therefore, a line that divides two sides of a triangle proportionally is parallel to the third side.

Proving the Pythagorean Theorem using similar triangles

To prove the Pythagorean Theorem for right $\triangle ABC$, show $(AB)^2 + (BC)^2 = (AC)^2$. Identify three similar triangles created by drawing altitude $\overline{BD}$. Use rotation and translation to verify that the three triangles are similar by AA. $\triangle ABC \sim \triangle BDC \sim \triangle ADB$. Similar triangles have proportional sides, so $\frac{AB}{AD} = \frac{AC}{AB}$ and $\frac{BC}{DC} = \frac{AC}{BC}$. Also note, $AD + DC = AC$.

Use cross multiplication:	$\frac{AB}{AD} = \frac{AC}{AB} \rightarrow (AB)^2 = (AD)(AC)$ $\frac{BC}{DC} = \frac{AC}{BC} \rightarrow (BC)^2 = (DC)(AC)$
Add these two new equations together:	$(AB)^2 + (BC)^2 = (AD)(AC) + (DC)(AC)$.
Use the distributive property to simplify the right side:	$(AB)^2 + (BC)^2 = (AD + DC)(AC)$
Use substitution:	$(AB)^2 + (BC)^2 = (AC)(AC)$
Simplify:	$(AB)^2 + (BC)^2 = (AC)^2$

(drawings not to scale)

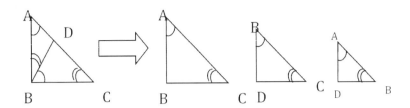

Using triangle congruence (ASA) to solve problems and prove relationships in geometric figures

Triangle congruence (ASA) can be used to solve problems involving triangles when two pairs of corresponding angles are known to be congruent and the contained sides are also congruent. To solve for the third angle, subtract the sum of the known angles from 180°. Once triangle congruence is established, all other corresponding parts of the triangles can also be identified as congruent.

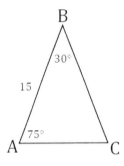 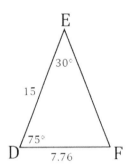

Given $\triangle ABC$ and $\triangle DEF$.
1. Show $\triangle ABC \cong \triangle DEF$.
2. Find the length of AC.
3. Find the measure of $\angle F$.

1. Since $m\angle A = m\angle D = 75°$, $AB = DE = 15$, and $m\angle B = m\angle E = 30°$, $\triangle ABC \cong \triangle DEF$ by Angle-Side-Angle Congruence.

2. Since corresponding parts of congruent triangles are congruent, $AC = DF = 7.76$.

3. Since the sum of the angles in a triangle is 180°, add the measure of $\angle D$ and the measure of $\angle E$ and subtract from 180°: $180° - (75° + 30°) = 180° - 105° = 75°$. $m\angle F = 75°$.

Using triangle congruence (SAS) to solve problems and prove relationships in geometric figures

Triangle congruence (SAS) can be used to solve problems involving triangles when two pairs of corresponding sides are known to be congruent and the contained angles are also congruent. Once triangle congruence is established, all other corresponding parts of the triangles can also be identified as congruent.

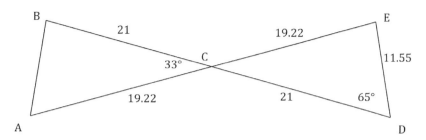

Given $\triangle ABC$ and $\triangle EDC$.

1. Show $\triangle ABC \cong \triangle EDC$.
2. Find the length of AB.
3. Find the measure of $\angle E$.

1. Since $BC = DC = 21$, $\angle BCA \cong \angle DCE$ (vertical angles), and $AC = EC = 19.22$, $\triangle ABC \cong \triangle DEF$ by Side-Angle-Side Congruence.

2. Since Corresponding Parts of Congruent Triangles are Congruent, $AB = ED = 11.55$.

3. The sum of the angles in a triangle is 180°.

$$\angle C + \angle D + \angle E = 180°$$

$$33° + 65° + \angle E = 180°$$

$$98° + \angle E = 180°$$

$$\angle E = 82°$$

Using triangle congruence (SSS) to solve problems and prove relationships in geometric figures

Triangle congruence (SSS) can be used to solve problems involving triangles when all pairs of corresponding sides are known to be congruent. Once triangle congruence is established, all other corresponding parts of the triangles can also be identified as congruent.

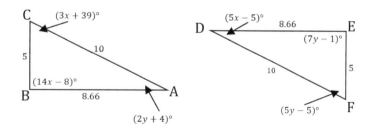

Given $\triangle ABC$ and $\triangle DEF$,

1. Show $\triangle ABC \cong \triangle DEF$.

2. Find the measure of $\angle D$.

3. Find the measure of $\angle E$.

4. Find the measure of $\angle F$.

1. Since $AB = DE = 8.66$, $BC = EF = 5$, and $AC = DF = 10$, $\triangle ABC \cong \triangle DEF$ by Side-Side-Side Congruence.

2. Since the sum of the angles in a triangle add to $180°$, write an equation for each triangle.

$\triangle ABC$:	$\triangle EDC$:
$(2y + 4) + (14x - 8) + (3x + 39)$ $= 180$ $17x + 2y + 35 = 180$ $17x + 2y = 145$ $y = \frac{145 - 17x}{2}$	$(5x - 5) + (5y - 5) + (7y - 1) = 180$ $5x + 12y - 11 = 180$ $5x + 12y = 191$

Solve the system of equations.

| $5x + 12\left(\frac{145 - 17x}{2}\right) = 191$ $5x + 870 - 102x = 191$ $-97x = -679$ $x = 7$ | $y = \frac{145 - 17(7)}{2}$ $y = \frac{145 - 119}{2} = \frac{26}{2}$ $y = 13$ |

$m\angle D = 5x - 5 = 5(7) - 5 = 35 - 5 = 30°$.

3. $m\angle E = 7y - 1 = 7(13) - 1 = 91 - 1 = 90°$.

4. $m\angle F = 5y - 5 = 5(13) - 5 = 65 - 5 = 60°$.

Using triangle similarity (AA) to solve problems and prove relationships in geometric figures

Triangle similarity (AA) can be used to solve problems involving triangles when two pairs of corresponding angles are known to be congruent. To solve for the third angle, subtract the sum of the known angles from $180°$. Once triangle similarity is established, all pairs of corresponding angles in the triangles can be identified as congruent and all pairs of corresponding sides in the triangles can be identified as proportional.

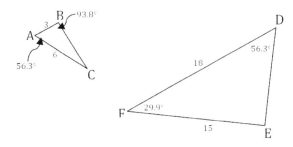

Given $\triangle ABC$ and $\triangle DEF$

- 28 -

1. Find the measure of $\angle E$.

2. Find the measure of $\angle C$.

3. Show $\triangle ABC \sim \triangle DEF$.

4. Find the length of DE.

5. Find the length of BC.

1. Since the sum of the angles of a triangle is 180°, $m\angle E = 180° - (29.9° + 56.3°) = 180° - 86.2° = 93.8°$.

2. Since the sum of the angles of a triangle is 180°, $m\angle C = 180° - (56.3° + 93.8°) = 180° - 150.1° = 29.9°$.

3. Since $m\angle A = m\angle D = 56.3°$ and $m\angle B = m\angle E = 93.8°$, $\triangle ABC \sim \triangle DEF$ by Angle-Angle Similarity.

4. Since corresponding sides are proportional in similar triangles, $\frac{AB}{DE} = \frac{AC}{DF}, \frac{3}{DE} = \frac{6}{18} \rightarrow 54 = 6 \cdot DE \rightarrow DE = 9$.

5. Since corresponding sides are proportional in similar triangles, $\frac{BC}{EF} = \frac{AC}{DF}, \frac{BC}{15} = \frac{6}{18} \rightarrow 18 \cdot BC = 90 \rightarrow BC = 5$.

Trigonometric ratio sine for an acute angle using ratios of sides in similar right triangles

Similar triangles have three pairs of congruent angles and three pairs of proportional sides. The proportion has the same value for all pairs of sides, so $\frac{a}{d} = \frac{c}{f}$ or (using cross multiplication and division to reorganize) $\frac{a}{c} = \frac{d}{f}$. The trigonometric ratio sine is opposite over hypotenuse. In $\triangle ABC$, $\sin A = \frac{a}{c}$ and in $\triangle DEF$, $\sin D = \frac{d}{f}$. So since $\frac{a}{c} = \frac{d}{f}$, $\sin A = \sin D$. This shows that the trigonometric ratio sine is a property of the angle because the ratio is the same in both triangles even though the triangles are different sizes.

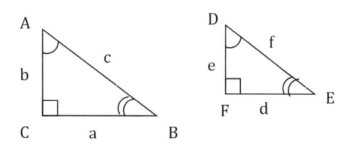

Trigonometric ratio cosine for an acute angle using ratios of sides in similar right triangles

Similar triangles have three pairs of congruent angles and three pairs of proportional sides. The proportion has the same value for all pairs of sides, so $\frac{b}{e} = \frac{c}{f}$ or (using cross multiplication and division to reorganize) $\frac{b}{c} = \frac{e}{f}$. The trigonometric ratio cosine is adjacent over hypotenuse. In $\triangle ABC$, $\cos A = \frac{b}{c}$ and in $\triangle DEF$, $\cos D = \frac{e}{f}$. So since $\frac{b}{c} = \frac{e}{f}$, $\cos A = \cos D$. This shows that the trigonometric ratio cosine is a property of the angle because the ratio is the same in both triangles even though the triangles are different sizes.

Trigonometric ratio tangent for an acute angle using ratios of sides in similar right triangles

Similar triangles have three pairs of congruent angles and three pairs of proportional sides. The proportion has the same value for all pairs of sides, so $\frac{a}{d} = \frac{b}{e}$ or (using cross multiplication and division to reorganize) $\frac{a}{b} = \frac{d}{e}$. The trigonometric ratio tangent is opposite over adjacent. In $\triangle ABC$, $\tan A = \frac{a}{b}$ and in $\triangle DEF$, $\tan D = \frac{d}{e}$. So since $\frac{a}{b} = \frac{d}{e}$, $\tan A = \tan D$. This shows that the trigonometric ratio tangent is a property of the angle because the ratio is the same in both triangles even though the triangles are different sizes.

Relationship between sine and cosine of complementary angles

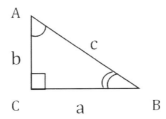

The sum of two complementary angles is 90°. In a right triangle, the two acute angles are complementary because the sum of the angles (180°) minus the right angle (90°) leaves the sum of the acute angles (90°). So, $m\angle A + m\angle B = 90°$. $\sin A = \frac{opp}{hyp} = \frac{a}{c}$ and $\cos B = \frac{adj}{hyp} = \frac{a}{c}$, thus the sine of an angle is equal to the cosine of its complementary angle.

Using sine to solve problems involving right triangles

Problems that can be solved using sine must give specific information and ask for a specific solution.

Given	Unknown
one acute angle and the side opposite that angle	the hypotenuse
one acute angle and the hypotenuse	the side opposite that angle
the hypotenuse and one leg	the angle opposite the known leg **to solve this problem, use $\sin^{-1}$**

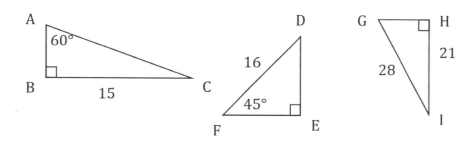

Given △ ABC, △ DEF, and △ GHI,

1. Solve for the length of the hypotenuse in ⊿ABC.
2. Solve for the length of DE in ⊿DEF.
3. Solve for the measure of ∠G in ⊿GHI.

1. In ⊿ABC, AC is the hypotenuse and $\sin A = \frac{BC}{AC}$. So, $\sin 60 = \frac{15}{AC} \rightarrow AC = \frac{15}{\sin 60} = 17.32$.

2. In ⊿DEF, $\sin F = \frac{DE}{DF}$. So, $\sin 45 = \frac{DE}{16} \rightarrow DE = 16 \cdot \sin 45 = 11.31$.

3. In ⊿GHI, $\sin G = \frac{HI}{GI}$. So, $\sin G = \frac{21}{28} \rightarrow G = \sin^{-1} \frac{21}{28} = 48.59°$.

Using cosine to solve problems involving right triangles

Problems that can be solved using cosine must give specific information and ask for a specific solution.

Given	Unknown
one acute angle and the side adjacent to that angle	the hypotenuse
one acute angle and the hypotenuse	the side adjacent to that angle
the hypotenuse and one side	the angle adjacent to the known side **to solve this problem, use $\cos^{-1}$**

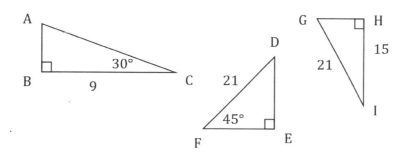

Given △ ABC, △ DEF, and △ GHI,

1. Solve for the length of the hypotenuse in $\triangle ABC$.

2. Solve for the length of EF in $\triangle DEF$.

3. Solve for the measure of $\angle I$ in $\triangle GHI$.

1. In $\triangle ABC$, AC is the hypotenuse and $\cos C = \frac{BC}{AC}$. So, $\cos 30 = \frac{9}{AC} \rightarrow AC = \frac{9}{\cos 30} = 10.39$.

2. In $\triangle DEF$, $\cos F = \frac{EF}{DF}$. So, $\cos 45 = \frac{EF}{21} \rightarrow EF = 21 \cdot \cos 45 = 14.85$.

3. In $\triangle GHI$, $\cos I = \frac{HI}{GI}$. So, $\cos I - \frac{15}{21} \rightarrow I - \cos^{-1} \frac{15}{21} = 44.42°$.

Using tangent to solve problems involving right triangles

Problems that can be solved using tangent must give specific information and ask for a specific solution.

Given	Unknown
one acute angle and the side opposite that angle	the side adjacent to that angle
one acute angle and the side adjacent to that angle	the side opposite that angle
two legs	either of the two acute angles **to solve this problem, use $\tan^{-1}$**

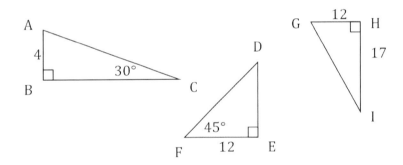

Given $\triangle ABC$, $\triangle DEF$, and $\triangle GHI$,

1. Solve for the length of BC in $\triangle ABC$.

2. Solve for the length of DE in $\triangle DEF$.

3. Solve for the measure of $\angle I$ in $\triangle GHI$.

1. In $\triangle ABC$, $\tan C = \frac{AB}{BC}$. So, $\tan 30 = \frac{4}{BC} \rightarrow BC = \frac{4}{\tan 30} = 6.93$.

2. In $\triangle DEF$, $\tan F = \frac{DE}{EF}$. So, $\tan 45 = \frac{DE}{12} \rightarrow DE = 12 \cdot \tan 45 = 12$.

3. In $\triangle GHI$, $\tan I = \frac{GH}{HI}$. So, $\tan I = \frac{12}{17} \rightarrow I = \tan^{-1} \frac{12}{17} = 35.22°$.

Using the Pythagorean Theorem to solve problems involving right triangles

Problems that can be solved using the Pythagorean Theorem must give specific information and ask for a specific solution.

Given	Unknown
two legs	the hypotenuse
one leg and the hypotenuse	the other leg

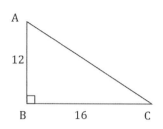 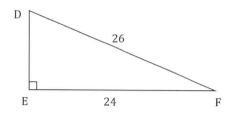

Given $\triangle ABC$ and $\triangle DEF$,

1. Solve for the length of AC in $\triangle ABC$.
2. Solve for the length of DE in $\triangle DEF$.

1. In $\triangle ABC$, $AB^2 + BC^2 = AC^2$. So, $12^2 + 16^2 = AC^2$ → $AC^2 = 144 + 256 = 400$ → $AC = \sqrt{400} = 20$.

2. In $\triangle DEF$, $DE^2 + EF^2 = DF^2$. So, $DE^2 + 24^2 = 26^2$ → $DE^2 + 576 = 676$ → $DE^2 = 676 - 576 = 100$ → $DE = \sqrt{100} = 10$

From the triangle area formula $Area = \frac{1}{2}bh$, where b is the length of triangle's base, and h is the triangle's height, derive the formula $Area_{\triangle ABC} = \frac{1}{2} \cdot a \cdot b \cdot \sin C$ by drawing an auxiliary line from a vertex perpendicular to the opposite side.

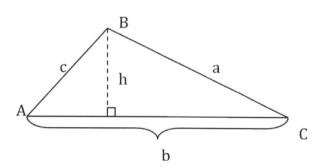

$Area_{\triangle ABC} = \frac{1}{2} \cdot b \cdot h$. Notice that h is an auxiliary line from the vertex, B, and perpendicular to the opposite side, AC, and h divides $\triangle ABC$ into two right triangles. From the triangle on the right, $\sin C = \frac{h}{a}$, so $h = a \cdot \sin C$. Substituting this into the area formula creates $Area_{\triangle ABC} = \frac{1}{2} \cdot b \cdot (a \cdot \sin C)$, which can be written $Area_{\triangle ABC} = \frac{1}{2} \cdot a \cdot b \cdot \sin C$.

Prove the Law of Sines

The Law of Sines states that for any $\triangle ABC$, $\frac{\sin A}{a} = \frac{\sin B}{b} = \frac{\sin C}{c}$. To prove this, draw an auxiliary line from the vertex at B, perpendicular to AC. Notice that $\sin A = \frac{h}{c}$, so $\frac{\sin A}{a} = \frac{\frac{h}{c}}{a} = \frac{h}{c} \cdot \frac{1}{a} = \frac{h}{a \cdot c}$. Notice that $\sin C = \frac{h}{a}$, so $\frac{\sin C}{c} = \frac{\frac{h}{a}}{c} = \frac{h}{a} \cdot \frac{1}{c} = \frac{h}{a \cdot c}$. Therefore, $\frac{\sin A}{a} = \frac{\sin C}{c}$.

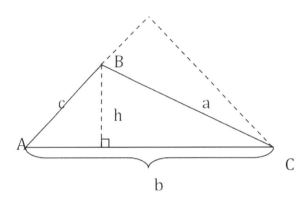

Now, draw an auxiliary line (call it g) from another vertex C) perpendicular to the opposite side AB to create two other right triangles. Notice that $\sin A = \frac{g}{b}$, so $\frac{\sin A}{a} = \frac{\frac{g}{b}}{a} = \frac{g}{b} \cdot \frac{1}{a} = \frac{g}{a \cdot b}$. Notice that $\sin B = \frac{g}{a}$, so $\frac{\sin B}{b} = \frac{\frac{g}{a}}{b} = \frac{g}{a} \cdot \frac{1}{b} = \frac{g}{a \cdot b}$. Therefore, $\frac{\sin A}{a} = \frac{\sin B}{b}$. Since $\frac{\sin A}{a} = \frac{\sin C}{c}$ and $\frac{\sin A}{a} = \frac{\sin B}{b}$ are both true, $\frac{\sin A}{a} = \frac{\sin B}{b} = \frac{\sin C}{c}$ is also true.

Prove the Law of Cosines

The Law of Cosines states: $c^2 = a^2 + b^2 - 2 \cdot a \cdot b \cdot \cos C$. To prove this, draw an auxiliary line from the vertex at B, perpendicular to AC. Side b is now split into two lengths, x and $b - x$.

use the Pythagorean Theorem to write an equation about the right triangle with hypotenuse a	$a^2 = x^2 + h^2$
use trigonometry to write a cosine equation about angle C	$\cos C = \frac{x}{a}$ $x = a \cdot \cos C$
use the Pythagorean Theorem two write an equation about the right triangle with hypotenuse c	$c^2 = (b - x)^2 + h^2$ $c^2 = (b^2 - 2 \cdot b \cdot x + x^2) + h^2$ $c^2 = b^2 - 2 \cdot b \cdot x + (x^2 + h^2)$
substitute a^2 for $(x^2 + h^2)$	$c^2 = b^2 - 2 \cdot b \cdot x + a^2$ $c^2 = a^2 + b^2 - 2 \cdot b \cdot x$
substitute $a \cdot \cos C$ for x	$c^2 = a^2 + b^2 - 2 \cdot b \cdot (a \cdot \cos C)$ $c^2 = a^2 + b^2 - 2 \cdot a \cdot b \cdot \cos C$

- 34 -

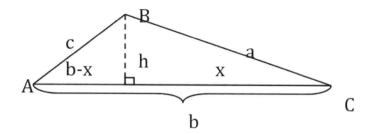

Using the Law of Sines to solve problems involving triangles

Problems that can be solved using the Law of Sines must give specific information and ask for a specific solution.

Given	Unknown
two sides and an angle opposite one side	the angle opposite the other side
two angles and a side (find the third angle using the Angle Sum Theorem if necessary)	the side opposite any angle

Given $\triangle ABC$ and $\triangle DEF$,

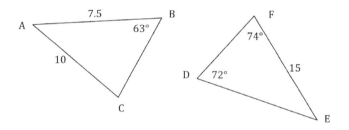

1. Find the measure of $\angle C$.

2. Find the measure of $\angle A$.

3. Find the length of BC.

4. Find the measure of $\angle E$.

5. Find the length of DE.

6. Find the length of DF.

1. $\frac{\sin C}{AB} = \frac{\sin B}{AC} \rightarrow \frac{\sin C}{7.5} = \frac{\sin 63}{10} \rightarrow \sin C = \frac{7.5 \cdot \sin 63}{10} = 0.668 \rightarrow C = \sin^{-1} 0.668 = 41.9°.$

2. Since the sum of the angles in a triangle is $180°$, $m\angle A = 180 - (63 + 41.9) = 180 - 104.9 = 75.1°.$

3. $\frac{\sin A}{BC} = \frac{\sin B}{AC} \rightarrow \frac{\sin 75.1}{BC} = \frac{\sin 63}{10} \rightarrow BC \cdot \sin 63 = 10 \cdot \sin 75.1 \rightarrow BC = \frac{10 \cdot \sin 75.1}{\sin 63} = 10.85.$

4. Since the sum of the angles in a triangle is $180°$, $m\angle E = 180 - (72 + 74) = 180 - 146 = 34°.$

5. $\frac{\sin F}{DE} = \frac{\sin D}{EF} \rightarrow \frac{\sin 74}{DE} = \frac{\sin 72}{15} \rightarrow DE \cdot \sin 72 = 15 \cdot \sin 74 \rightarrow DE = \frac{15 \cdot \sin 74}{\sin 72} = 15.16.$

6. $\frac{\sin E}{DF} = \frac{\sin D}{EF} \rightarrow \frac{\sin 34}{DF} = \frac{\sin 72}{15} \rightarrow DF \cdot \sin 72 = 15 \cdot \sin 34 \rightarrow DF = \frac{15 \cdot \sin 34}{\sin 72} = 8.82.$

- 35 -

Using the Law of Cosines to solve problems involving triangles.

Problems that can be solved using the Law of Cosines must give specific information and ask for a specific solution.

Given	Unknown	Form of the Equation
two sides and the angle between them	the third side	$c^2 = a^2 + b^2 - 2 \cdot a \cdot b \cdot \cos C$
three sides	any angle	$\cos C = \dfrac{a^2 + b^2 - c^2}{2 \cdot a \cdot b}$

Given $\triangle ABC$ and $\triangle DEF$, use the Law of Cosines to

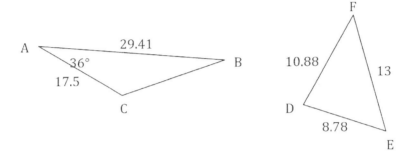

1. Find the length of BC.
2. Find the measure of $\angle B$.
3. Find the measure of $\angle C$.
4. Find the measure of $\angle D$.
5. Find the measure of $\angle E$.
6. Find the measure of $\angle F$.

1. $BC^2 = AB^2 + AC^2 - 2 \cdot AB \cdot AC \cdot \cos A = (29.41)^2 + (17.5)^2 - 2 \cdot (29.41) \cdot (17.5) \cdot \cos 36 = 338.436 \rightarrow BC = \sqrt{338.436} = 18.40$

2. $\cos B = \frac{AB^2 + BC^2 - AC^2}{2 \cdot AB \cdot BC} = \frac{29.41^2 + 18.4^2 - 17.5^2}{2 \cdot 29.41 \cdot 18.4} = 0.829 \rightarrow B = \cos^{-1} 0.829 = 34°.$

3. $\cos C = \frac{BC^2 + AC^2 - AB^2}{2 \cdot BC \cdot AC} = \frac{18.4^2 + 17.5^2 - 29.41^2}{2 \cdot 18.4 \cdot 17.5} = -0.342 \rightarrow C = \cos^{-1} -0.342 = 110°.$

4. $\cos D = \frac{DE^2 + DF^2 - EF^2}{2 \cdot DE \cdot DF} = \frac{8.78^2 + 10.88^2 - 13^2}{2 \cdot 8.78 \cdot 10.88} = 0.139 \rightarrow D = \cos^{-1} 0.139 = 82.04°.$

5. $\cos E = \frac{DE^2 + EF^2 - DF^2}{2 \cdot DE \cdot EF} = \frac{8.78^2 + 13^2 - 10.88^2}{2 \cdot 8.78 \cdot 13} = 0.559 \rightarrow E = \cos^{-1} 0.559 = 55.98°.$

6. $\cos F = \frac{DF^2 + EF^2 - DE^2}{2 \cdot DF \cdot EF} = \frac{10.88^2 + 13^2 - 8.78^2}{2 \cdot 10.88 \cdot 13} = 0.743 \rightarrow F = \cos^{-1} 0.743 = 41.98°.$

Use the Law of Sines and the illustration to solve the following problem:

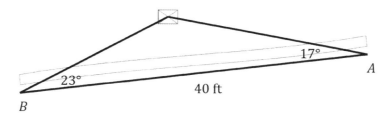

Bob is camping near a river. Bob walks upstream and finds a place to cross the river (point A). Then he turns and walks along stream for 40 feet until he is past the camp and at another river crossing (point B). How far is Bob from the tent at each crossing?

The Law of Sines is used to solve for an unknown side when two angles and one of the sides opposite an angle are known. In this problem, it is possible to find the third angle, which is opposite the known side, and use it to solve for the two missing side lengths.

$m\angle tent = 180 - (23 + 17) = 180 - 40 = 140°$.

$\frac{\sin tent}{AB} = \frac{\sin B}{b} \rightarrow \frac{\sin 140}{40} = \frac{\sin 23}{b} \rightarrow b \cdot \sin 140 = 40 \cdot \sin 23 \rightarrow b = \frac{40 \cdot \sin 23}{\sin 140} = 23.31$. The distance from the tent to the first crossing is 23.31 feet.

$\frac{\sin tent}{AB} = \frac{\sin A}{a} \rightarrow \frac{\sin 140}{40} = \frac{\sin 17}{a} \rightarrow a \cdot \sin 140 = 40 \cdot \sin 17 \rightarrow a = \frac{40 \cdot \sin 17}{\sin 140} = 18.19$. The distance from the second crossing to the tent is 18.19 feet.

Use the Law of Sines to solve the following problem:

Seth is building a tree house in a 15-foot tree on a hill in his backyard. At the base of the tree are rosebushes, which his mother will not let him remove. Seth has decided to build a 23.7-foot ladder from the base of the hill to the top of the tree. If the tree meets the ground at a 115° angle, at what angle will the ladder meet the hill?

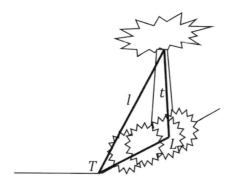

The Law of Sines is used to solve for an angle when another angle and the two sides opposite those angles are known.

$\frac{\sin L}{l} = \frac{\sin T}{t} \rightarrow \frac{\sin 115}{23.7} = \frac{\sin T}{15} \rightarrow 23.7 \cdot \sin T = 15 \cdot \sin 115 \rightarrow \sin T = \frac{15 \cdot \sin 115}{23.7} = 0.574 \rightarrow T = \sin^{-1} 0.574 = 35°$

The ladder will meet the hill at an angle of 35°.

- 37 -

Use the Law of Cosines to solve the following problem:

Sally is flying her plane on the heading shown in the figure. The plane's instrument panel indicates an air speed of 140 mph. However, there is a crosswind of 53 mph. What is the apparent speed (x) of the plane to an observer on the ground?

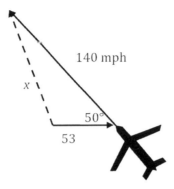

The Law of Cosines is used to solve for the third side in a triangle when two sides and the angle between them are known.

$$x^2 = (53)^2 + (140)^2 - 2 \cdot 53 \cdot 140 \cdot \cos 50 = 12870.03 \rightarrow x = \sqrt{12870.03} = 113.45 \text{ mph.}$$

Use the Law of Cosines to solve the following problem:

Beth is returning to her campsite from an ATV ride when she remembers she still has to pay for the campsite. Earlier, she entered the locations of her campsite and the ranger station into her GPS. The GPS tells her that she is 5 miles from her tent and 8 miles from the ranger station. If Beth also knows that her tent is 4 miles from the ranger station, how many degrees must she alter her course to pay the bill before returning to her campsite?

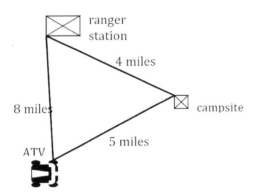

The Law of Cosines is used to solve for an angle in a triangle when three sides are known.

$$\cos A = \frac{AR^2 + AC^2 - CR^2}{2 \cdot AR \cdot AC} = \frac{8^2 + 5^2 - 4^2}{2 \cdot 8 \cdot 5} = 0.9125 \rightarrow A = \cos^{-1} 0.9125 = 24.15°.$$

Beth must alter her course by 24.15° toward the ranger station to reach the ranger station.

Circles

Proving that all circles are similar

Similar figures have the same shape but not necessarily the same size. Similar polygons have congruent corresponding angles and proportional sides. To extend this idea to circles, consider an arbitrary number of points along the circle. If points are chosen in such a way that the angles created by the radii to those points are congruent when measured from a horizontal radius, then the corresponding angles are congruent. If the ratios of corresponding radii are found and compared, the results would be proportional, thus all circles are similar.

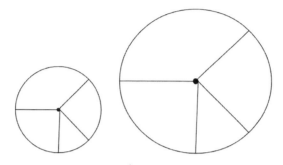

Relationship between (1) central angles and inscribed angles and (2) central angles and circumscribed angles

All of these angles have rays which pass through the same points on the circle at B and C. A central angle's vertex is at the same point as the center of a circle. An inscribed angle's vertex is on a point on the circle. A circumscribed angle's vertex is outside the circle, and its rays are tangent to the circle.

$$m\angle BDC = \frac{1}{2} \cdot m\angle BAC$$

$$m\angle BEC = 180 - m\angle BAC$$

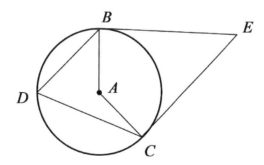

Relationship between inscribed angles whose endpoints lie on a diameter. Relationship between a tangent and the radius at the point of tangency

The measure of all inscribed angles is equal to half the intercepted arc. Since a diameter creates an arc of 180°, all inscribed angles whose endpoints lie on a diameter have a measure of 90°, are right angles, and are congruent.

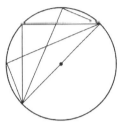

A tangent intersects a circle at only one point. The radius is a line segment from the center of the circle to a point on a circle. A tangent is perpendicular to the radius at the point of tangency.

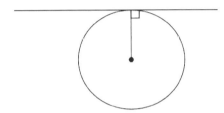

Construction of a circle inscribed in a triangle

Given a triangle, construct the angle bisectors of each of its angles. Place the compass tip on one of the vertices, open the compass and draw an arc that intersects both rays of the angle. Open the compass a little further and move the stationary end to one of the side-arc intersections. Make a small arc beyond the first arc. Without changing the compass opening, move the stationary end to the other side-arc intersection. Make another small arc that intersects the last small arc. Use a straightedge to draw a line through the angle vertex and the point of intersection for the two small arcs. Repeat these steps for the other two vertices of the triangle.

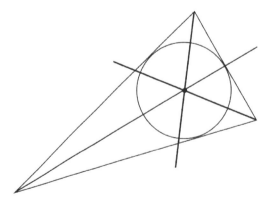

The point where the three angle bisectors intersect is called the incenter. The incenter is equidistant from all three sides of the triangle.

Because each of a triangle's sides is be tangent to an inscribed circle, the circle's radius is perpendicular to each side. Draw a line from the incenter which is perpendicular to one of the triangle's sides. Place the compass tip on the incenter and adjust the width so that two arcs can be drawn on one of the sides of the triangle. Without changing the compass width, place the tip on one of the side-arc intersections and draw an arc outside the triangle; then, place the tip on the other side-arc intersection and draw an arc which intersects the first. Use a straightedge to connect this point of intersection to the incenter.

To draw the circle, position the tip on the compass at the incenter and adjust the compass width to meet the triangle's side where it is crossed by the constructed perpendicular. Draw a circle inside the triangle, noting that the circle touches the triangle once on each side.

Construction of a circle circumscribed around a triangle

Construct the perpendicular bisector of each side of the triangle. Place the compass tip on one of the vertices, open the compass past the middle of the side, and draw an arc that extends both inside and outside the triangle. Without changing the compass opening, move to the other endpoint of the side and draw another arc that intersects the first. Use the straightedge to draw the line that connects the two intersections of the arcs and that is perpendicular to the side it bisects. Repeat these steps for the other two sides of the triangle.

The point where the perpendicular bisectors intersect is called the circumcenter. The circumcenter is equidistant from all three vertices of the triangle. Place the compass tip on the circumcenter and open the compass so the pencil is touching one of the vertices. Draw a circle around the triangle, noting that the circle touches the triangle at each of its vertices.

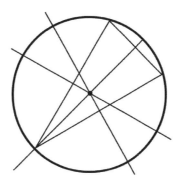

Prove the sum of the measures of opposite angles in a quadrilateral inscribed in a circle is 180°.

Since quadrilateral $ABCD$ is inscribed in circle P, angles A, B, C, and D are all inscribed in circle P.

The measure of an inscribed angle is equal to half the arc it intercepts. Angle A intercepts $\widehat{BCD}$ and angle C intercepts $\widehat{DAB}$	$m\angle A = \dfrac{1}{2} \cdot m\widehat{BCD} \;\rightarrow\; m\widehat{BCD} = 2 \cdot m\angle A$ $m\angle C = \dfrac{1}{2} \cdot m\widehat{DAB} \;\rightarrow\; m\widehat{DAB} = 2 \cdot m\angle C$
$\widehat{BCD}$ and $\widehat{DAB}$ are two arcs that form a whole circle.	$m\widehat{BCD} + m\widehat{DAB} = 360°$
Use substitution.	$2 \cdot m\angle A + 2 \cdot m\angle C = 360°$
Use the distributive property and divide by 2.	$2 \cdot (m\angle A + m\angle C) = 360°$ $m\angle A + m\angle C = 180°$

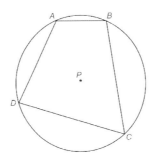

Construct a tangent line from a point outside a circle to the circle.

Consider $\odot C$ and a point A outside of circle C. First, use a straightedge to construct $\overline{AC}$. Find M, the midpoint of $\overline{AC}$. Place the compass tip on point M and draw a circle through C. These two points of intersection (points B and D) are both points of tangency. Use a straightedge to construct a line through either point of tangency and point A. This line is tangent to circle C from a point outside the circle.

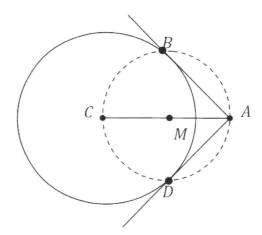

Using similarity to show the length of an arc intercepted by a central angle is proportional to the radius

Consider two concentric circles, $\odot C$ with radius r and $\odot C$ with radius R. $\angle ACB$ cuts an arc $(\overset{\frown}{AB})$ in the larger circle and a similar arc $(\overset{\frown}{DE})$ in the smaller circle. The circumference of a circle is $2\pi r$ and an arc is a piece of the circle. The measure of the central angle determines what fraction the arc is of the circle. So, to find the length of the arc, multiply the fraction and the circumference.

In degrees, $l\overset{\frown}{AB} = \frac{m\angle C}{360} \cdot 2\pi R$. In radians, $l\overset{\frown}{AB} = \frac{m\angle C}{2\pi} \cdot 2\pi R = m\angle C \cdot R$.

In degrees, $l\overset{\frown}{DE} = \frac{m\angle C}{360} \cdot 2\pi r$. In radians, $l\overset{\frown}{DE} = \frac{m\angle C}{2\pi} \cdot 2\pi r = m\angle C \cdot r$.

Using radians, $\frac{l\overset{\frown}{AB}}{R} = m\angle C$ and $\frac{l\overset{\frown}{DE}}{r} = m\angle C$, so $\frac{l\overset{\frown}{AB}}{R} = \frac{l\overset{\frown}{DE}}{r}$. The lengths of the arcs are proportional to the lengths of the radii.

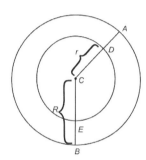

Using similarity to define radian measure of a central angle as the constant of proportionality

Consider two concentric circles, $\odot C$ with radius r and $\odot C$ with radius R. $\angle ACB$ cuts an arc $(\overset{\frown}{AB})$ in the larger circle and a similar arc $(\overset{\frown}{DE})$ in the smaller circle. The lengths of the arcs are proportional to the lengths of the radii: $\frac{l\overset{\frown}{AB}}{R} = \frac{l\overset{\frown}{DE}}{r}$.

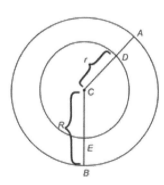

$$l\widehat{AB} = \frac{m\angle C}{2\pi} \cdot 2\pi R = m\angle C \cdot R \ \rightarrow \ \frac{l\widehat{AB}}{R} = m\angle C.$$

$$l\widehat{DE} = \frac{m\angle C}{2\pi} \cdot 2\pi r = m\angle C \cdot r \rightarrow \frac{l\widehat{DE}}{r} = m\angle C.$$

Looking at the equations, $\frac{l\widehat{AB}}{R} = m\angle C$ and $\frac{l\widehat{DE}}{r} = m\angle C$, so the constant of the proportion is the radian measure of angle C.

Deriving the formula for the area of a sector

The area of $\odot C$ is πr^2. A circle has 360° and a sector is a slice of the circle. The measure of the central angle determines what fraction the sector is of the circle. So, to find the area of the sector, multiply the fraction and the area of the whole circle.

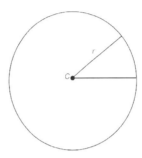

In degrees, $Area_{sector} = \frac{m\angle C}{360} \cdot \pi r^2$.

In radians, $Area_{sector} = \frac{m\angle C}{2\pi} \cdot \pi r^2 = \frac{m\angle C}{2} \cdot r^2$.

Expressing Geometric Properties with Equations

Deriving the equation of a circle with a given center and radius using the Pythagorean Theorem

Given is a circle with center (h, k) and radius r. Point (x, y) is on the circle. Use the Pythagorean Theorem to determine a relationship between the distance r and the points (h, k) and (x, y). In the right triangle, the length of the horizontal leg is $(x - h)$ and the length of the vertical leg is $(y - k)$. The Pythagorean Theorem states that the square of the hypotenuse is equal to the sum of the squares of the legs, or $(x - h)^2 + (y - k)^2 = r^2$. This equation defines the circle with center (h, k), radius r, and point (x, y) on the circle.

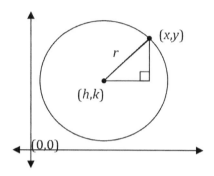

Finding the equation of a circle with center $(-2, 8)$ and radius $r = 6$ using the Pythagorean Theorem

Given a circle with center $(-2, 8)$ and radius $r = 6$. Point (x, y) is on the circle. Use the Pythagorean Theorem to determine a relationship between the distance $r = 6$ and the points $(-2, 8)$ and (x, y). In the right triangle, the length of the horizontal leg is $(x + 2)$ and the length of the vertical leg is $(y - 8)$. The Pythagorean Theorem states that the square of the hypotenuse is equal to the sum of the squares of the legs, or $(x - h)^2 + (y - k)^2 = r^2 \rightarrow (x + 2)^2 + (y - 8)^2 = 6^2 \rightarrow (x + 2)^2 + (y - 8)^2 = 36$.

Use completing the square to find the center and radius of a circle given by the polynomial equation: $x^2 + y^2 + 6x - 2y - 6 = 0$

In a polynomial of the form $Ax^2 + By^2 + Cx + Dy + E = 0$, the equation defines a circle when $A = B$.

Rewrite the equation by grouping the x-terms and y-terms and moving the constant to the other side of the equation.	$x^2 + y^2 + 6x - 2y - 6 = 0$ $(x^2 + 6x) + (y^2 - 2y) = 6$
Prepare to complete the square by adding spaces in each set of parentheses and on the other side of the equation.	$(x^2 + 6x + \_) + (y^2 - 2y + \_)$ $= 6 + \_ + \_$

- 45 -

For the x group: $\left(\frac{6}{2}\right)^2 =$ $3^2 = 9$ For the y group: $\left(\frac{2}{2}\right)^2 =$ $1^2 = 1$	Determine what is added to each group by dividing the middle coefficient by 2 and then squaring the result.	$(x^2 + 6x + 9) + (y^2 - 2y + 1) = 6 + 9 + 1$
	Factor the groups and simplify the right side of the equation.	$(x + 3)^2 + (y - 1)^2 = 16$
	Identify h, k, and r.	$x - h = x + 3 \ \rightarrow h = -3$ $y - k = y - 1 \ \rightarrow k = 1$ $r^2 = 16 \ \rightarrow r = 4$

The center of the circle is (-3, 1), and the radius is 4.

Identify the equation of a parabola given a focus and directrix

1. focus: (2,5) and directrix: $y = 1$

2. focus: $(6, -2)$ and directrix: $x = 0$

A parabola is the set of points equidistant from a point called the focus and line called the directrix, which does not pass through the focus. A parabola curves around the focus and away from the directrix but intersects neither. The vertex (h, k) of the parabola lies on the parabola's line of symmetry, which passes through the focus and is perpendicular to the directrix.

1. Identify the orientation of the parabola. Since the directrix is a horizontal line represented by the equation $y = 1$, the parabola is oriented vertically and can therefore be represented by the equation $4p(y - k) = (x - h)^2$, where (h, k) is the vertex of the parabola and $(h, k + p)$ is the focus of the parabola. The vertex is halfway between the focus and the directrix, so find the mean of the y-values in the focus and directrix to find the vertex: $\left(2, \frac{5+1}{2}\right) \rightarrow (2,3) = (h, k)$. The y-value of the focus, 5, is represented by $k + p$; $k = 3$, so $3 + p = 5 \rightarrow p = 2$. Substitute h, k, and p into the equation of a parabola: $4p(y - k) = (x - h)^2 \ \rightarrow 8(y - 3) = (x - 2)^2$.

2. Identify the orientation of the parabola. Since the directrix is a vertical line represented by the equation $x = 0$, the parabola is oriented horizontally and can therefore be represented by the equation $4p(x - h) = (y - k)^2$, where (h, k) is the vertex of the parabola and $(h + p, k)$ is the focus of the parabola. The vertex is halfway between the focus and the directrix, so find the mean of the x-values in the focus and directrix to find the vertex: $\left(\frac{6+0}{2}, -2\right) \rightarrow (3, -2)$. Compare the x-values in the vertex and the focus to find p: $p = 6 - 3 = 3$. Substitute h, k, and p into the equation of a parabola: $4p(x - h) = (y - k)^2 \ \rightarrow 12(x - 3) = (y + 2)^2$.

Identify the equation of an ellipse with foci at $(5, 3)$ and $(11, 3)$ and a focal constant of 10

An ellipse is the set of points around two foci such that the sum of the distances from any point on the ellipse to each focus is the focal constant. The center of the ellipse is equidistant from the foci and lies on the major axis. The orientation of the ellipse is also along the major axis. The ends of the major axis are called vertices. The ends of the minor axis are called co-vertices.

Identify the orientation of the ellipse. The y-values are the same in both foci, so the major axis of the ellipse is at $y = 3$. Therefore, the ellipse is oriented horizontally. The equation for an ellipse with a

- 46 -

horizontal major axis is $\frac{(x-h)^2}{a^2} + \frac{(y-k)^2}{b^2} = 1$, where (h,k) is the center of the ellipse, a is half the focal constant, and a and b are related by the equation $a^2 - b^2 = c^2$, where c is the horizontal distance between the focus and the center.

The center is the point along the major axis between the two foci: $\left(\frac{11+5}{2}, 3\right) \rightarrow (8,3)$. Find the horizontal distance c between the focus and the center: $c = 11 - 8 = 3$. Divide the focal constant by 2 to find a: $a = \frac{10}{2} = 5$. Find b by using a, c, and the formula $a^2 - b^2 = c^2$: $5^2 - b^2 = 3^2 \rightarrow 25 - b^2 = 9 \rightarrow b^2 = 25 - 9 = 16 \rightarrow b = 4$. Substitute $a, b, h,$ and k into the equation of an ellipse: $\frac{(x-h)^2}{a^2} + \frac{(y-k)^2}{b^2} = 1 \rightarrow \frac{(x-8)^2}{5^2} + \frac{(y-3)^2}{4^2} = 1 \rightarrow \frac{(x-8)^2}{25} + \frac{(y-3)^2}{16} = 1$.

Identify the equation of an ellipse with foci at $(2,1)$ and $(2,5)$ and a focal constant of 5

An ellipse is the set of points around two foci such that the sum of the distances from any point on the ellipse to each focus is the focal constant. The center of the ellipse is equidistant from the foci and lies on the major axis. The orientation of the ellipse is also along the major axis. The ends of the major axis are called vertices. The ends of the minor axis are called co-vertices.

Identify the orientation of the ellipse. The x-values are the same in both foci, so the major axis of the ellipse is at $x = 2$. Therefore, the ellipse is oriented vertically. The equation for an ellipse with a horizontal major axis is $\frac{(x-h)^2}{b^2} + \frac{(y-k)^2}{a^2} = 1$, where (h,k) is the center of the ellipse, a is half the focal constant, and a and b are related by the equation $a^2 - b^2 = c^2$, where c is the vertical distance between the focus and the center.

The center is the point along the major axis between the two foci: $\left(2, \frac{1+5}{2}\right) \rightarrow (2,3)$. Find the vertical distance c between the focus and the center: $c = 5 - 3 = 2$. Divide the focal constant by 2 to find a: $a = \frac{5}{2} = 2.5$. Find b by using a, c, and the formula $a^2 - b^2 = c^2$: $(2.5)^2 - b^2 = 2^2 \rightarrow 6.25 - b^2 = 4 \rightarrow b^2 = 6.25 - 4 = 2.25 \rightarrow b = 1.5$. Substitute $a, b, h,$ and k into the equation of an ellipse: $\frac{(x-h)^2}{b^2} + \frac{(y-k)^2}{a^2} = 1 \rightarrow \frac{(x-2)^2}{1.5^2} + \frac{(y-3)^2}{2.5^2} = 1 \rightarrow \frac{(x-2)^2}{2.25} + \frac{(y-3)^2}{6.25} = 1 \rightarrow \frac{(x-2)^2}{\frac{9}{4}} + \frac{(y-3)^2}{\frac{25}{4}} = 1 \rightarrow \frac{4(x-2)^2}{9} + \frac{4(y-3)^2}{25} = 1$

Identify the equation of a hyperbola given the foci $(-4,5)$ and $(6,5)$ and focal constant 8

A hyperbola is the set of points whose distances from the foci are different by a constant (the focal constant). The foci are two points, one in each section of the hyperbola. The center, (h,k), is a point between the two sections of the hyperbola and is equidistant from the foci and along the major axis.

To find the equation of the hyperbola, first identify the orientation of the hyperbola. The foci lie along the line $y = 5$, so the hyperbola is orientated horizontally. The center is the point equidistant from the foci: $\left(\frac{-4+6}{2}, 5\right) \rightarrow (1,5)$. Compare the x-values of the center and one focus to find c: $c = 1 - (-4) = 5$. Divide the focal constant by 2 to find a: $a = \frac{8}{2} = 4$. Find b by using a, c, and the formula $a^2 + b^2 = c^2$: $4^2 + b^2 = 5^2 \rightarrow 16 + b^2 = 25 \rightarrow b^2 = 25 - 16 = 9 \rightarrow b = 3$. Substitute a, $b, h,$ and k into the equation of a horizontally oriented hyperbola: $\frac{(x-h)^2}{a^2} - \frac{(y-k)^2}{b^2} = 1 \rightarrow \frac{(x-1)^2}{4^2} - \frac{(y-5)^2}{3^2} = 1 \rightarrow \frac{(x-1)^2}{16} - \frac{(y-5)^2}{9} = 1$.

Identify the equation of a hyperbola with foci at $(-2, -4)$ and $(-2, 22)$ and a focal constant of 10

A hyperbola is the set of points whose distances from the foci are different by a constant (the focal constant). The foci are two points, one in each section of the hyperbola. The center, (h, k), is a point between the two sections of the hyperbola and is equidistant from the foci and along the major axis.

To find the equation of the hyperbola, first identify the orientation of the hyperbola. The foci lie along the line $x = -2$, so the hyperbola is orientated vertically. The center is the point equidistant from the foci: $\left(-2, \frac{-4+22}{2}\right) \rightarrow (-2, 9)$. Compare the y-values of the center and one focus to find c: $c = 22 - 9 = 13$. Divide the focal constant by 2 to find a: $a = \frac{10}{2} = 5$. Find b by using a, c, and the formula $a^2 + b^2 = c^2$: $5^2 + b^2 = 13^2 \rightarrow 25 + b^2 = 169 \rightarrow b^2 = 169 - 25 = 144 \rightarrow b = 12$. Substitute a, b, h, and k into the equation of a vertically oriented hyperbola: $\frac{(y-k)^2}{a^2} - \frac{(x-h)^2}{b^2} = 1 \rightarrow \frac{(y-9)^2}{5^2} - \frac{(x+2)^2}{12^2} = 1 \rightarrow \frac{(y-9)^2}{25} - \frac{(x+2)^2}{144} = 1$.

Determine whether or not the quadrilateral defined by $A(5,4)$, $B(-4,3)$, $C(-4,1)$, and $D(5,1)$ is a rectangle

A rectangle has two pairs of congruent opposite sides and four right angles. To find the lengths of the sides, use the distance formula, $d = \sqrt{(x_1 - x_2)^2 + (y_1 - y_2)^2}$.

AB	BC
$\sqrt{[5 - (-4)]^2 + (4 - 3)^2}$	$\sqrt{[-4 - (-4)]^2 + (3 - 1)^2}$
$\sqrt{(9)^2 + (1)^2}$	$\sqrt{(0)^2 + (2)^2}$
$\sqrt{81 + 1}$	$\sqrt{0 + 4}$
$\sqrt{82}$	$\sqrt{4} = 2$
CD	DA
$\sqrt{(-4 - 5)^2 + (1 - 1)^2}$	$\sqrt{(5 - 5)^2 + (1 - 4)^2}$
$\sqrt{(-9)^2 + (0)^2}$	$\sqrt{(0)^2 + (-3)^2}$
$\sqrt{81 + 0}$	$\sqrt{0 + 9}$
$\sqrt{81} = 9$	$\sqrt{9} = 3$

Since $AB \neq CD$ and $BC \neq DA$, Quadrilateral $ABCD$ is not a rectangle, and no further testing is required.

Determine whether or not the quadrilateral defined by $A(8, -1)$, $B(-2, -1)$, $C(-2,6)$, and $D(8,6)$ is a rectangle

A rectangle has two pairs of congruent opposite sides and four right angles. To find the lengths of the sides, use the distance formula, $d = \sqrt{(x_1 - x_2)^2 + (y_1 - y_2)^2}$.

AB	BC
$\sqrt{[8 - (-2)]^2 + [-1 - (-1)]^2}$	$\sqrt{[-2 - (-2)]^2 + (-1 - 6)^2}$
$\sqrt{(10)^2 + (0)^2}$	$\sqrt{(0)^2 + (-7)^2}$
$\sqrt{100 + 0}$	$\sqrt{0 + 49}$
$\sqrt{100} = 10$	$\sqrt{49} = 7$

- 48 -

$$
\begin{array}{c}
CD \\
\sqrt{(-2-8)^2 + (6-6)^2} \\
\sqrt{(-10)^2 + (0)^2} \\
\sqrt{100 + 0} \\
\sqrt{100} = 10
\end{array}
\qquad
\begin{array}{c}
DA \\
\sqrt{(8-8)^2 + [6-(-1)]^2} \\
\sqrt{(0)^2 + (7)^2} \\
\sqrt{0 + 49} \\
\sqrt{49} = 7
\end{array}
$$

Since $AB = CD$ and $BC = DA$, Quadrilateral $ABCD$ might be a rectangle, and further testing is required. To determine if the angles are right angles, find the slopes of the four sides. Perpendicular sides will have opposite, inverse slopes.

$$
\begin{array}{c}
AB \\
m = \dfrac{(-1)-(-1)}{(-2)-8} = \dfrac{0}{-10} = 0 \\
CD \\
m = \dfrac{6-6}{8-(-2)} = \dfrac{0}{10} = 0
\end{array}
\qquad
\begin{array}{c}
BC \\
m = \dfrac{6-(-1)}{(-2)-(-2)} = \dfrac{7}{0} = undef \\
DA \\
m = \dfrac{(-1)-6}{(-2)-(-2)} = \dfrac{-7}{0} = undef
\end{array}
$$

Although $\overline{BC}$ and $\overline{DA}$ have undefined slopes, they are perpendicular to $\overline{AB}$ and $\overline{CD}$ because lines with undefined slopes are perpendicular to lines with slopes of 0.

Determine whether or not the point $(3,3\sqrt{3})$ lies on the circle which is centered at the origin and which contains the point $(0,6)$

To check that a point lies on a circle, find the radius, r, of the circle using the given point and center, (h,k). $x = 0$ $y = 6$ $h = 0$ $k = 0$	$(x-h)^2 + (y-k)^2 = r^2$ $(0-0)^2 + (6-0)^2 = r^2$ $(0)^2 + (6)^2 = r^2$ $0 + 36 = r^2$ $36 = r^2$ $6 = r$
Then check to see if the point lies on a circle with the same center and radius. $x = 3$ $y = 3\sqrt{3}$ $h = 0$ $k = 0$	$(x-h)^2 + (y-k)^2 = r^2$ $(3-0)^2 + \left(3\sqrt{3}-0\right)^2 = r^2$ $(3)^2 + \left(3\sqrt{3}\right)^2 = r^2$ $9 + 27 = r^2$ $36 = r^2$ $6 = r$

The two circles have the same center $(0,0)$ and the same radius $r = 6$, so both the point $(3,3\sqrt{3})$ lies on the circle which is centered at the origin and which contains the point $(0,6)$.

Determine whether or not the point $(1,2)$ **lies on the circle which is centered at the origin and which contains the point** $(\sqrt{2}, \sqrt{2})$

To check that a point lies on a circle, find the radius, r, of the circle using the given point and center, (h, k). $$x = \sqrt{2}$$ $$y - \sqrt{2}$$ $$h = 0$$ $$k = 0$$	$$(x - h)^2 + (y - k)^2 = r^2$$ $$\left(\sqrt{2} - 0\right)^2 + \left(\sqrt{2} - 0\right)^2 = r^2$$ $$\left(\sqrt{2}\right)^2 + \left(\sqrt{2}\right)^2 = r^2$$ $$2 + 2 = r^2$$ $$4 = r^2$$ $$2 = r$$
Then check to see if the point lies on a circle with the same center and radius. $$x = 1$$ $$y = 2$$ $$h = 0$$ $$k = 0$$	$$(x - h)^2 + (y - k)^2 = r^2$$ $$(1 - 0)^2 + (2 - 0)^2 = r^2$$ $$(1)^2 + (2)^2 = r^2$$ $$1 + 4 = r^2$$ $$5 = r^2$$ $$\sqrt{5} = r$$

The point $(1,2)$ does not lie on the circle which is centered at the origin and which contains the point $(\sqrt{2}, \sqrt{2})$.

Show that the lines given by equations $5y + 2x = 7$ **and** $10y + 4x = 28$ **are parallel**

Parallel lines are two lines which have the same slope and do not intersect. To determine whether $5y + 2x = 7$ and $10y + 4x = 28$ are parallel, first find the slope of each line by rewriting in slope-intercept form: $5y = -2x + 7 \rightarrow y = \frac{-2}{5}x + \frac{7}{5}$; $10y = -4x + 28 \rightarrow y = \frac{-4}{10}x + \frac{28}{10} \rightarrow y = \frac{-2}{5}x + \frac{14}{5}$. The two lines have same slope. To show the lines do not intersect, show that there is no solution to the system formed by the given equations. $\frac{-2}{5}x + \frac{7}{5} = \frac{-2}{5}x + \frac{14}{5} \rightarrow \frac{7}{5} = \frac{14}{5}$. When the solution of a system of equations results in a false statement, the solution is the empty set; there is no point contained by both lines, so the lines do not intersect.

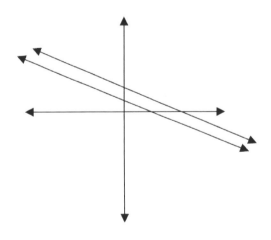

Show that the lines given by equations $y - 3x = 5$ and $3y + x = -6$ are perpendicular

When two lines have slopes which are negative reciprocals of each other. ($m_1 \cdot m_2 = -1$), they are perpendicular, which means they meet at right angles.

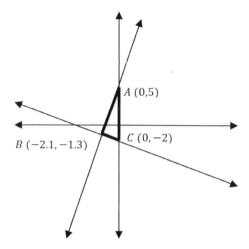

Find the slope of the given two lines, $y - 3x = 5$ and $3y + x = -6$, by rewriting in slope-intercept form: $y = 3x + 5$; $3y = -x - 6 \rightarrow y = \frac{-1}{3}x - \frac{6}{3} \rightarrow y = \frac{-1}{3}x - 2$. The two lines have slopes $m_1 = 3$ and $m_2 = \frac{-1}{3}$, which are negative reciprocals. Therefore, the lines are perpendicular.

Find the equation of the line passing through $(-2, 6)$ and parallel to $5y - 15x = -25$

Parallel lines have the same slopes.

Given equation: $5y - 15x = -25$
$$5y = 15x - 25$$
$$y = 3x - 5$$
Slope: $m_1 = 3 = m_2$

Solution equation: $y = m \cdot x + b$
$(y = 6, m_2 = 3, x = -2)$
$$6 = 3 \cdot (-2) + b$$
$$6 = -6 + b$$
$$12 = b$$

$$y = 3x + 12$$
$$y - 3x = 12$$

The line passing through $(-2,6)$ and parallel to $5y - 15x = -25$ is $y - 3x = 12$.

- 51 -

Find the equation of the line passing through $(9, -1)$ and perpendicular to $-2y + 3x = 5$

Perpendicular lines have opposite, inverse slopes.

Given equation: $-2y + 3x = 5$
$$-2y = -3x + 5$$
$$y = \frac{-3}{-2}x + 5$$
$$y = \frac{3}{2}x + 5$$
Slope: $m_1 = \frac{3}{2}$
$$m_1 \cdot m_2 = -1$$
$$\frac{3}{2} \cdot m_2 = -1$$
$$m_2 = \frac{-2}{3}$$

Solution equation: $y = m \cdot x + b$
$(y = -1, m_2 = \frac{-2}{3}, x = 9)$
$$-1 = \frac{-2}{3} \cdot 9 + b$$
$$-1 = -6 + b$$
$$5 = b$$

$$y = \frac{-2}{3} \cdot x + 5$$
$$3y = -2x + 15$$
$$3y + 2x = 15$$

The line passing through $(9, -1)$ and perpendicular to $-2y + 3x = 5$ is $3y + 2x = 15$.

Find the point that partitions a given line segment into two segments with a given length ratio.

Given two points, (x_1, y_1) and (x_2, y_2) and the ratio $a{:}b$.

steps:	x-values:	y-values:
find the difference between the values	$d_x = x_2 - x_1$	$d_y = y_2 - y_1$
find the fraction that represents the ratio	$a{:}b \to \frac{a}{a+b}$ this is the fraction of difference between x_1 and x_3	$a{:}b \to \frac{a}{a+b}$ this is also the fraction of difference between y_1 and y_3
find the difference between the first point and the partition point, multiply the fraction and the differences between x_1 and x_2 and y_1 and y_2	$m = \frac{a}{a+b} \cdot d_x$	$n = \frac{a}{a+b} \cdot d_y$
find the partition point by adding the differences to the first point	$x_3 = x_1 + m$	$y_3 = y_1 + n$

Find the point that partitions the line segment between $(3,4)$ and $(7,12)$ into two segments with a length ratio of $1{:}3$

Given two points, $(3,4)$ and $(7,12)$ and ratio $1{:}3$.

steps:	x-values:	y-values:
find the difference between the values	$d_x = 7 - 3 = 4$	$d_y = 12 - 4 = 8$
find the fraction that represents the ratio	$1{:}3 \to \frac{1}{1+3} = \frac{1}{4}$ this is the fraction of difference between x_1 and x_3	$1{:}3 \to \frac{1}{1+3} = \frac{1}{4}$ this is also the fraction of difference between y_1 and y_3

find the difference between the first point and the partition point, multiply the fraction and the differences between x_1 and x_2 and y_1 and y_2	$m = \frac{1}{4} \cdot 4 = 1$	$n = \frac{1}{4} \cdot 8 = 2$
find the partition point by adding the differences to the first point	$x_3 = 3 + 1 = 4$	$y_3 = 4 + 2 = 6$

The partition point is (4,6).

Find the point that partitions the line segment between $(-3,5)$ **and** $(3,-7)$ **into two segments with a length ratio of** $5:1$.

Given two points, $(-3,5)$ and $(3,-7)$ and ratio $5:1$.

steps:	x-values:	y-values:
find the difference between the values	$d_x = 3 - (-3) = 6$	$d_y = (-7) - 5 = -12$
find the fraction that represents the ratio	$5:1 \rightarrow \frac{5}{5+1} = \frac{5}{6}$ this is the fraction of difference between x_1 and x_3	$5:1 \rightarrow \frac{5}{5+1} = \frac{5}{6}$ this is also the fraction of difference between y_1 and y_3
find the difference between the first point and the partition point, multiply the fraction and the differences between x_1 and x_2 and y_1 and y_2	$m = \frac{5}{6} \cdot 6 = 5$	$n = \frac{5}{6} \cdot (-12) = -10$
find the partition point by adding the differences to the first point	$x_3 = -3 + 5 = 2$	$y_3 = 5 + (-10) = -5$

The partition point is $(2, -5)$.

Using coordinates to find the perimeter of a figure

Find the distance between all vertices. Add all the distances together.
$$d_{AB} = \sqrt{(x_B - x_A)^2 + (y_B - y_A)^2}$$

Using coordinates to find the area of a figure

Find the critical distances. Use the appropriate formula.

for TRIANGLES:
find the *BASE* and the *HEIGHT*
the height may not be along the side of the triangle
use the formula: $AREA = \frac{1}{2} \cdot BASE \cdot HEIGHT$

for RECTANGLES:
find the *LENGTH* and the *WIDTH*
use the formula: $AREA = LENGTH \cdot WIDTH$

Find the perimeter of the figure given by the points $A(5,4)$, $B(3,-1)$, and $C(7,-1)$

$$d_{AB} = \sqrt{(3-5)^2 + (-1-4)^2} = \sqrt{(-2)^2 + (-5)^2} = \sqrt{4+25} = \sqrt{29}$$

$$d_{BC} = \sqrt{(7-3)^2 + [-1-(-1)]^2} = \sqrt{(4)^2 + (0)^2} = \sqrt{16+0} = \sqrt{16} = 4$$

$$d_{CA} = \sqrt{(5-7)^2 + [4-(-1)]^2} = \sqrt{(-2)^2 + (5)^2} = \sqrt{4+25} = \sqrt{29}$$

Perimeter: $d_{AB} + d_{BC} + d_{CA} = \sqrt{29} + 4 + \sqrt{29} = 4 + 2\sqrt{29}$.

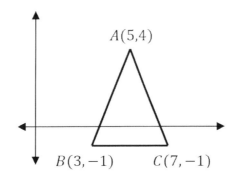

Find the perimeter of the figure given by the points $A(7,11)$, $B(3,3)$, $C(9,0)$ and $D(13,8)$

$$d_{AB} = \sqrt{(3-7)^2 + (3-11)^2} = \sqrt{(-4)^2 + (-8)^2} = \sqrt{16+64} = \sqrt{80} = 4\sqrt{5}$$

$$d_{BC} = \sqrt{(9-3)^2 + (0-3)^2} = \sqrt{(6)^2 + (-3)^2} = \sqrt{36+9} = \sqrt{45} = 3\sqrt{5}$$

$$d_{CD} = \sqrt{(13-9)^2 + (8-0)^2} = \sqrt{(4)^2 + (8)^2} = \sqrt{16+64} = \sqrt{80} = 4\sqrt{5}$$

$$d_{DA} = \sqrt{(7-13)^2 + (11-8)^2} = \sqrt{(-6)^2 + (3)^2} = \sqrt{36+9} = \sqrt{45} = 3\sqrt{5}$$

Perimeter: $d_{AB} + d_{BC} + d_{CD} + d_{DA} = 4\sqrt{5} + 3\sqrt{5} + 4\sqrt{5} + 3\sqrt{5} = 2(4\sqrt{5}) + 2(3\sqrt{5}) = 8\sqrt{5} + 6\sqrt{5} = 14\sqrt{5}$.

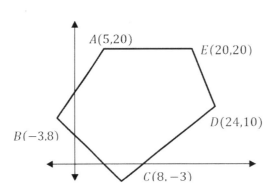

- 54 -

Find the perimeter of the figure given by the points $A(5, 20)$, $B(-3, 8)$, $C(8, -3)$, $D(24, 10)$ and $E(20, 20)$.

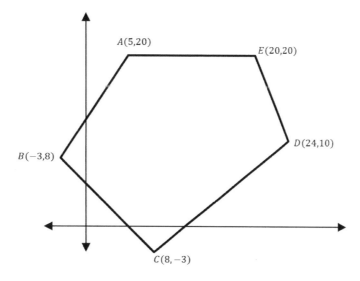

$$d_{AB} = \sqrt{(-3-5)^2 + (8-20)^2} = \sqrt{(-8)^2 + (-12)^2} = \sqrt{64+144} = \sqrt{208} = 4\sqrt{13}$$

$$d_{BC} = \sqrt{[8-(-3)]^2 + (-3-8)^2} = \sqrt{(11)^2 + (-11)^2} = \sqrt{121+121} = \sqrt{242} = 11\sqrt{2}$$

$$d_{CD} = \sqrt{(24-8)^2 + [10-(-3)]^2} = \sqrt{(16)^2 + (13)^2} = \sqrt{256+169} = \sqrt{425} = 5\sqrt{17}$$

$$d_{DE} = \sqrt{(20-24)^2 + (20-10)^2} = \sqrt{(-4)^2 + (10)^2} = \sqrt{16+100} = \sqrt{116} = 2\sqrt{29}$$

$$d_{EA} = \sqrt{(5-20)^2 + (20-20)^2} = \sqrt{(-15)^2 + (0)^2} = \sqrt{225+0} = \sqrt{225} = 15$$

Perimeter: $d_{AB} + d_{BC} + d_{CD} + d_{DE} + d_{EA} = 4\sqrt{13} + 11\sqrt{2} + 5\sqrt{17} + 2\sqrt{29} + 15$.

Find the area of the figure given by the points $A(5, 4)$, $B(3, -1)$, and $C(7, -1)$

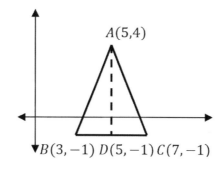

$BASE = d_{BC} = \sqrt{(7-3)^2 + [-1-(-1)]^2} = \sqrt{(4)^2 + (0)^2} = \sqrt{16+0} = \sqrt{16} = 4$

The *HEIGHT* is the line segment through A and perpendicular to $\overline{BC}$.

$HEIGHT = d_{AD} = \sqrt{(5-5)^2 + (-1-4)^2} = \sqrt{(0)^2 + (-5)^2} = \sqrt{0+25} = \sqrt{25} = 5$

- 55 -

$$AREA = \frac{1}{2} \cdot BASE \cdot HEIGHT = \frac{1}{2} \cdot 4 \cdot 5 = \frac{1}{2} \cdot 20 = 10$$

The area of the triangle is 10 square units.

Find the area of the figure given by the points $A(7, 11)$, $B(3, 3)$, and $C(13, 8)$.

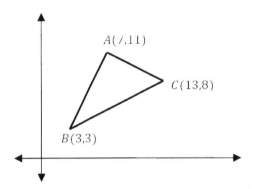

$$BASE = d_{AC} = \sqrt{(13 - 7)^2 + (8 - 11)^2} = \sqrt{(6)^2 + (-3)^2} = \sqrt{36 + 9} = \sqrt{45} = 3\sqrt{5}$$

$\overline{AC} \perp \overline{AB}$ because $m_{AB} \cdot m_{AC} = \frac{11-8}{7-13} \cdot \frac{11-3}{7-3} = \frac{3}{-6} \cdot \frac{8}{4} = \frac{24}{-24} = -1.$

$$HEIGHT = d_{AB} = \sqrt{(3 - 7)^2 + (3 - 11)^2} = \sqrt{(-4)^2 + (-8)^2} = \sqrt{16 + 64} = \sqrt{80} = 4\sqrt{5}$$

$$AREA = \frac{1}{2} \cdot BASE \cdot HEIGHT = \frac{1}{2} \cdot 3\sqrt{5} \cdot 4\sqrt{5} = \frac{1}{2} \cdot 12 \cdot 5 =$$

$$\frac{1}{2} \cdot 60 = 30$$

The area of the triangle is 30 square units.

Find the area of the figure given by the points $A(7, 11)$, $B(3, 3)$, $C(9, 0)$ and $D(13, 8)$.

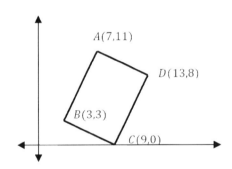

$$LENGTH = d_{AB} = \sqrt{(3 - 7)^2 + (3 - 11)^2} = \sqrt{(-4)^2 + (-8)^2} = \sqrt{16 + 64} = \sqrt{80} = 4\sqrt{5}$$

$\overline{AB} \perp \overline{AD}$ because $m_{AB} \cdot m_{AD} = \frac{11-3}{7-3} \cdot \frac{11-8}{7-13} = \frac{8}{4} \cdot \frac{3}{-6} = \frac{24}{-24} = -1.$

$$WIDTH = d_{AD} = \sqrt{(13 - 7)^2 + (8 - 11)^2} = \sqrt{(6)^2 + (-3)^2} =$$

$$\sqrt{36 + 9} = \sqrt{45} = 3\sqrt{5}$$

$$AREA = LENGTH \cdot WIDTH = 4\sqrt{5} \cdot 3\sqrt{5} = 12 \cdot 5 = 60$$

The area of the rectangle is 60 square units.

Geometric Measurement and Dimension

Formula for the circumference of a circle

Use transformations to show the ratio between the diameter of a circle and the distance around the circle is a constant, π: $\frac{C_\odot}{d} = \pi$. As the circle is rotated and translated, the circle moves along the line that is just over three times the length of the diameter.

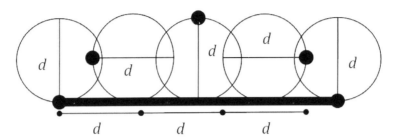

$C_\odot = \pi d = 2\pi r$.

Formula for the area of a circle

Use dissection to show that narrow sectors of the circle can be arranged to fit inside a parallelogram with height r and base πr. Using an informal limit, as the number of sectors increases and approaches a very large number, the dissection becomes more accurate and the difference between the area of the parallelogram and the area of the circle will get smaller.

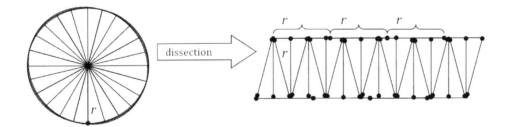

$A_\odot = \pi r^2$.

Formula for the volume of a cylinder

Using Cavalieri's principle, consider a cylinder and all the planes which intersect that cylinder parallel to the base. In each plane, there is a circle congruent to all the other circles in all the other planes. Since the circles are all congruent, they all have the same dimensions and the same areas. When all those circles are stacked together, the resulting solid, the cylinder, has a volume equal to the height of the stack times the area of the base.

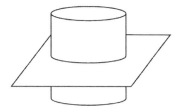

$V_{cylinder} = B \cdot h = \pi r^2 h.$

Formula for the volume of a pyramid

Consider a pyramid and a prism with the same altitude and the same base. The area of the prism is $A_{prism} = B \cdot h$ where B is the area of the base and h is the length of the altitude. Notice in the figures, that the pyramid appears to be inside the prism; this indicates that the volume of the pyramid will be less than the volume of the prism. Also notice that there are three different pyramids inside the prism. The first pyramid uses the front vertical edge as its altitude. The second pyramid uses the left vertical edge as its altitude. The third pyramid is the most difficult to see because it is between the other two. The third pyramid uses the right vertical edge as its altitude.

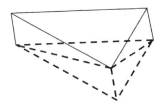 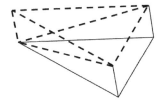 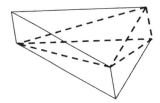

Since there are three pyramids inside the prism, all with the same base and the same altitude, the volume of each pyramid is $\frac{1}{3}$ the volume of the entire prism.

$A_{pyramid} = \frac{1}{3} B \cdot h.$

Formula for the volume of a cone

A pyramid and a cone are similar solids because the cross sections of both become smaller and smaller as they are taken farther and farther from the base.

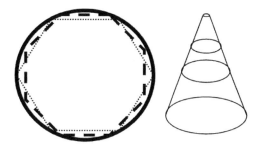

The volume of a pyramid is $\frac{1}{3} B \cdot h$ where B is the area of the base. If the base of a pyramid is a polygon with n sides, then, using an informal limit, as n increases and approaches a very large

- 59 -

number, the shape of the base begins to be like a circle. As shown in the figure to the right, even the change from 6 sides to 8 sides makes a much closer approximation of a circle. So the volume of a cone is also $\frac{1}{3}B \cdot h$ where $B = \pi r^2$.

$$V_{cone} = \frac{1}{3}B \cdot h = \frac{1}{3}\pi r^2 h.$$

Formula for the volume of a sphere

Consider a cross section of the sphere, not at the center: a circle with radius, c. This circle is a specific distance a from the center of the sphere. These two distances form a right triangle with the radius of the sphere which goes from the center of the sphere to the edge of the circle, so $a^2 + c^2 = r^2$ or $c^2 = r^2 - a^2$. The area of the cross section can be written as a function of the height and radius within the sphere. $A_{cross\ section} = \pi c^2 = \pi(r^2 - a^2) = \pi r^2 - \pi a^2$.

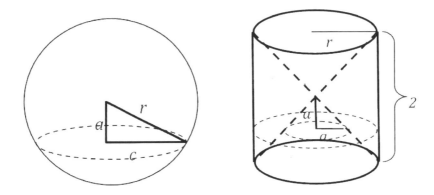

Consider also a cross section of cylinder with from which two congruent cones with tips touching in the cylinder's center have been removed. Again, let a represent the distance of the cross section's center from the center of the cylinder. The cross section through the cylinder is a circle with radius r from which a circle of radius a has been removed: $A_{cross\ section} = \pi r^2 - \pi a^2$.

Notice that the areas of the cross sections are the same. By Cavalieri's principle, the volumes of the sphere and of the cylinder with cones removed are therefore also the same. The volume of the cylinder without the cones removed is $V = Bh = \pi r^2(2r) = 2\pi r^3$. The volume of each cone is $V = \frac{1}{3}Bh = \frac{1}{3}\pi r^2(r) = \frac{1}{3}\pi r^3$. So, the volume of the cylinder with both cones removed, and therefore the volume of the sphere with radius r, is $2\pi r^3 - 2\left(\frac{1}{3}\pi r^3\right) = \frac{6}{3}\pi r^3 - \frac{2}{3}\pi r^3 = \frac{4}{3}\pi r^3$.

Cavalieri's principle

Cavalieri's principle states that the volumes of two solids are the same if the areas of their corresponding cross sections are equal.

- 60 -

Find the measure of the radius and the height in the cylinder shown if its volume is 603.186 cubic inches.

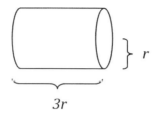

$$3r$$

$V_{cylinder} = \pi r^2 h = 603.186$ | $h = 3r = 3(4) = 12$
$\pi r^2 (3r) = 603.186$
$3\pi r^3 = 603.186$
$\pi r^3 = 201.062$
$r^3 = 64$
$r = 4$

The radius of the cylinder is 4 inches. The height of the cylinder is 12 inches.

Find the volume of the pyramid shown if the base is a square with sides $7\ yds$ long.

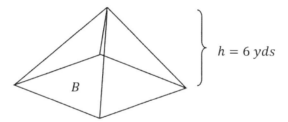

$h = 6\ yds$

B

$V_{pyramid} = \frac{1}{3} \cdot Bh = \frac{1}{3} \cdot s^2 h = \frac{1}{3} \cdot 7^2 \cdot 6 = \frac{1}{3} \cdot 49 \cdot 6 = \frac{1}{3} \cdot 294 = 98$

The volume of the pyramid is 98 cubic yards.

Find the amount of batter (in cubic cm) needed to create the ice cream cone shown.

The amount of batter needed is the volume of the solid. The volume is found by subtracting the volume of the inner cone from the volume of the outer cone.

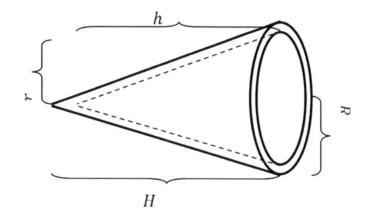

h

r

R

H

$$V_{outer\ cone} = \frac{1}{3} \cdot \pi R^2 H$$

$$V_{outer\ cone} = \frac{1}{3} \cdot \pi \cdot (2.5)^2 \cdot 10$$

$$V_{outer\ cone} = \frac{1}{3} \cdot \pi \cdot 6.25 \cdot 10$$

$$V_{outer\ cone} = \frac{1}{3} \cdot \pi \cdot 62.5$$

$$V_{outer\ cone} = \pi \cdot 20.833$$

$$V_{outer\ cone} = 65.45$$

$$V_{inner\ cone} = \frac{1}{3} \cdot \pi r^2 h$$

$$V_{inner\ cone} = \frac{1}{3} \cdot \pi \cdot 2^2 \cdot 9.5$$

$$V_{inner\ cone} = \frac{1}{3} \cdot \pi \cdot 4 \cdot 9.5$$

$$V_{inner\ cone} = \frac{1}{3} \cdot \pi \cdot 38$$

$$V_{inner\ cone} = \pi \cdot 12.667$$

$$V_{inner\ cone} = 39.79$$

$$V_{ice\ cream\ cone} = 65.45 - 39.79$$

$$V_{ice\ cream\ cone} = 25.66$$

25.66 cubic centimeters of batter is needed to create the ice cream cone.

Find the diameter of a sphere, in feet, if the volume of the sphere is 195,432.196 cubic inches

$V_{sphere} = \frac{4}{3} \cdot \pi r^3 = 195{,}432.196$ $\pi r^3 = 143{,}574.147$ $r^3 = 46656$ $r = 36$	$d = 2r = 2(36) = 72\ in$ $72\ in \cdot \dfrac{1\ ft}{12\ in} = 6\ ft$

The diameter of the sphere is 6 feet.

Name the vertical, horizontal, and slant cross sections for each of the solids shown

	right cylinder	sphere	right cone	double napped cone	triangular prism
vertical cross section	rectangle	circle	triangle	two triangles	rectangle
horizontal cross section	circle	circle	circle	circle	triangle
slant cross section	figure with two opposite sides parallel and two opposite sides curved	circle	ellipse OR parabola	ellipse OR parabola OR hyperbola	triangle

- 62 -

Name the vertical, horizontal, and slant cross sections for each of the solids shown

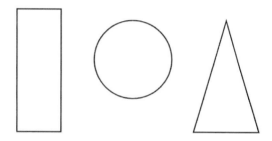

	triangular pyramid	rectangular prism	right pentagonal prism
vertical cross section	triangle	rectangle	pentagon
horizontal cross section	triangle	rectangle	rectangle
slant cross section	quadrilateral OR triangle	rectangle	rectangle

Name the solid created by rotating each of the figures shown around a vertical line through the center of the figure

Two dimensional figure	Three-dimensional figure
rectangle	cylinder
circle	sphere
isosceles triangle	cone

- 63 -

Modeling with Geometry

Name geometric shapes that can be used to model the following objects. Describe the properties of the shapes that make it a good model

1. the human torso
2. the human head
3. a coffee mug
4. an iPod
5. a book
6. a tire
7. an apple
8. a piece of string cheese
9. a log

1. The human torso can be modeled using a cylinder. The torso is round with a flat top (shoulders) and a flat bottom (hips).

2. The human head can be modeled using a sphere. The head is round in all directions.

3. A coffee mug can be modeled using a smaller cylinder inside a larger cylinder, aligned at the top. A coffee mug is round with a flat top and bottom.

4. An iPod can be modeled using a shallow rectangular prism. An iPod has two large, flat, rectangular sides (front and back) and four small, rectangular sides (top, bottom, left and right).

5. A book can be modeled on a rectangular prism. A book has six rectangular sides.

6. A tire can be modeled using a smaller cylinder inside a larger cylinder, centered. A tire is round with two flat sides.

7. An apple can be modeled using a sphere. An apple is a round orb.

8. A piece of string cheese can be modeled using a cylinder. A piece of string cheese is round with two flat ends.

9. A log can be modeled using a cylinder. A log is round with two flat ends.

The following table lists the four states with the largest populations in 2010 and the area (in square miles) of each state. Find the population density of each and list the states from highest to lowest population density.

State	2010 Population	Area (square miles)
California	37,253,956	158,648
Texas	25,145,561	266,874
New York	19,378,102	49,112
Florida	18,801,310	58,681

California:
$$\frac{37,253,956}{158,648} \approx 235 \text{ people/sq. mi}$$

Texas:
$$\frac{25,145,561}{266,874} \approx 94 \text{ people/sq. mi}$$

New York:
$$\frac{19,378,102}{49,112} \approx 395 \text{ people/sq. mi}$$

Florida:
$$\frac{18,801,310}{58,681} \approx 320 \text{ people/sq. mi}$$

Highest population density: New York, Florida, California.

Lowest population density: Texas.

The following table lists the four states with the smallest populations in 2010 and the area (in square miles) of each state. Find the population density of each and list the states from highest to lowest population density

State	2010 Population	Area (square miles)
Alaska	710,231	587,878
North Dakota	672,591	70,704
Vermont	625,741	9,615
Wyoming	563,626	97,818

Alaska:
$\frac{710,231}{587,878} \approx 1$ person/sq. mi

North Dakota:
$\frac{672,591}{70,704} \approx 10$ people/sq. mi

Vermont:
$\frac{625,741}{9,615} \approx 65$ people/sq. mi

Wyoming:
$\frac{563,626}{97,818} \approx 6$ people/sq. mi

Highest population density: Vermont, North Dakota, Wyoming.

Lowest population density: Alaska.

Salvador needs to determine if a medallion is made of pure gold. He knows the density of gold is 19.3 g/cm^3 and that the medallion weighs 250 g. Salvador submerges the medallion in a cylindrical container of water with a radius of 3 cm. Determine how many centimeters should the water rise to prove the medallion is pure gold

Let x=the volume of a 250 g gold medallion
$$\frac{19.3 \ g}{1 \ cm^3} = \frac{250 \ g}{x \ cm^3}$$
$$19.3 \cdot x = 250 \cdot 1$$
$$x = \frac{250}{19.3}$$
$$x = 12.95$$
The medallion has a volume of 12.95 cm^3 and should therefore displace 12.95cm^3 of water.

h=the change in height of water after medallion added
$$V = \pi r^2 h$$
$$12.95 = \pi \cdot 3^2 \cdot h$$
$$12.95 = 9\pi \cdot h$$
$$0.46 = h$$
The water will rise 0.46 cm if the medallion is made of pure gold.

A lump of metal, part nickel and part copper, weighs 1000 g. Valerie knows the ratio of nickel to copper is $2:3$. The density of nickel is 8.89 g/cm^3, and the density of copper is 8.97 g/cm^3.

- 65 -

Determine how many centimeters the water will rise when Valerie places the lump into a square prism container of water with sides 6 cm long

Nickel:

Weight: $\frac{2}{5} \cdot 1000 \text{ g} = 400 \text{ g}$

Displacement: $400 \text{ g} \cdot \frac{1 \text{ cm}^3}{8.89 \text{ g}} =$
44.99 cm^3

Copper:

Weight: $\frac{3}{5} \cdot 1000 \text{ g} = 600 \text{ g}$

Displacement: $600 \text{ g} \cdot \frac{1 \text{ cm}^3}{8.97 \text{ g}} =$
66.89 cm^3

Total Displacement: $44.99 \text{ cm}^3 + 66.89 \text{ cm}^3 = 111.88 \text{ cm}^3$

$$V_s = s^2 \cdot h$$
$$111.88 = 6^2 \cdot h$$
$$111.88 = 36 \cdot h$$
$$3.108 = h$$

The water level will rise 3.108 cm.

A factory cuts large sheets of cardstock (100 in by 102 in) into cards (3 in by 5 in). Determine the maximum number of cards the factory can cut and which side of the cards should be cut from the 100 in side of the sheets

Area of the large sheet:
$A_{sheet} = l \cdot w = 100 \cdot 102 = 10200$ square inches

Area of one card:
$A_{card} = l \cdot w = 3 \cdot 5 = 15$ square inches

Number of cards made:
$\frac{10200}{15} = 680$

Option 1: 3 in side cut from 100 in side

$\frac{100}{3} = 33.3333 \rightarrow 99$ in used and 33 cards per side

$\frac{102}{5} = 20.4 \rightarrow 100$ in used and 20 cards per side

$33 \cdot 20 = 660$ cards total

Option 2: 5 in side cut from the 100 in side

$\frac{100}{5} = 20 \rightarrow 100$ in used and 20 cards per side

$\frac{102}{3} = 34 \rightarrow 102$ in used and 34 cards per side

$34 \cdot 20 = 680$ cards total

Option 2 should be used to achieve the maximum number of cards made and avoid any wasted material.

A display box is designed to hold a single baseball so the ball touches all six faces of the box. If the diameter of a baseball is 2.9 in, how much empty space is in the box around the ball

$$V_{box} = s^3 = 2.9^3 = 24.389$$

$$V_{ball} = \frac{4}{3} \cdot \pi r^3 = \frac{4}{3} \cdot \pi \cdot (1.45)^3 = 12.77$$

$$V_{space} = V_{box} - V_{ball} = 24.389 - 12.77$$
$$= 11.619$$

The box has 11.619 cubic inches of space around the baseball.

Practice Test #1

Practice Questions

1. Which of the following statements is the definition of parallel lines?

    a. Two distinct coplanar lines that intersect at a 90°angle.
    b. Two distinct coplanar lines that do not intersect.
    c. Two rays with a common endpoint that point in opposite directions.
    d. Two rays sharing a common endpoint.

2. The definition "a function that takes points in the plane as inputs and gives other points as outputs" refers to which of the following terms?

    a. Coincident
    b. Invariant
    c. Mensuration
    d. Transformation

3. If trapezoid **JKLM**, shown below, was rotated 180° clockwise about the origin, determine which notation would represent the new coordinates of **J′K′L′M′**?

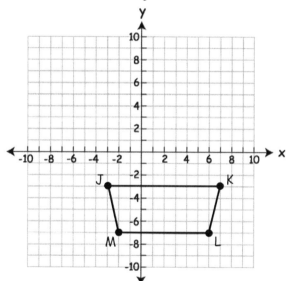

    a. $(x, y) \rightarrow (-x, -y)$
    b. $(x, y) \rightarrow (y, -x)$
    c. $(x, y) \rightarrow (-y, x)$
    d. $(x, y) \rightarrow (y, x)$

4. Which of the following figures show parallelogram **WXYZ** being carried onto its image **W'X'Y'Z'** by a reflection across the x-axis?

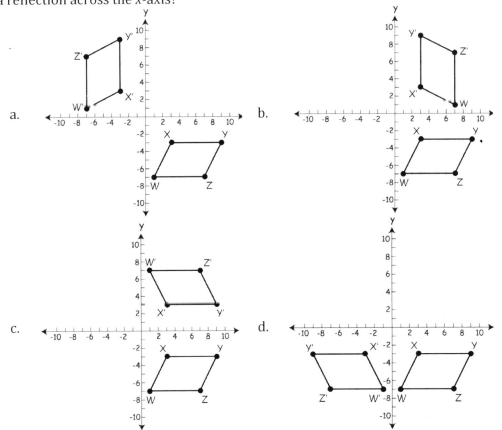

a.

b.

c.

d.

5. If $\overline{ST}$ is reflected across the line $y = x$, what is the new coordinate point of T'?

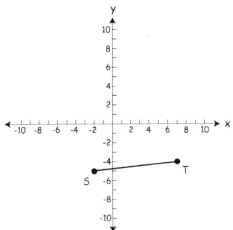

a. $(7, 4)$
b. $(-7, -4)$
c. $(4, -7)$
d. $(-4, 7)$

6. Which of the following figures has been rotated 90° clockwise about the origin?

a.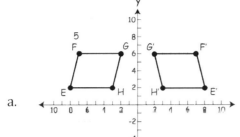

b.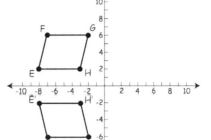

c.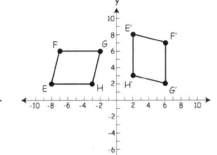

d.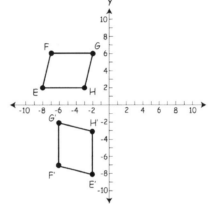

7. Which of the following rules describes the translation of **JKLM** to its image **J′K′L′M′**?

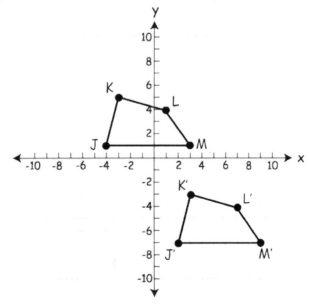

a. $(x, y) \rightarrow (x - 6, y + 8)$
b. $(x, y) \rightarrow (x + 6, y - 8)$
c. $(x, y) \rightarrow (x - 8, y + 6)$
d. $(x, y) \rightarrow (x + 8, y - 6)$

- 69 -

8. Which set of figures is congruent?

a.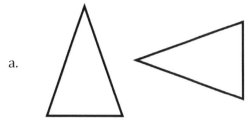

b.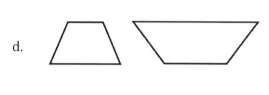

c.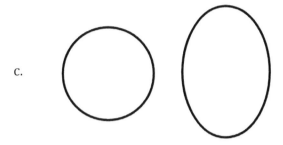

d.

9. Which of the following is true about the relationship between the two triangles shown below?

    a. The triangles are similar.
    b. The triangles are congruent.
    c. The triangles are equilateral.
    d. Both Answer A and Answer B are true.

10. ASA triangle congruence can be used to prove which of the following pairs of triangles congruent?

a.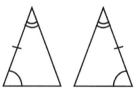

b.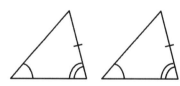

c.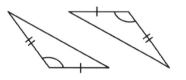

d.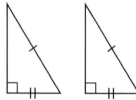

- 70 -

11. In the figure below, lines *a* and *b* are parallel. Find the value of *x*.

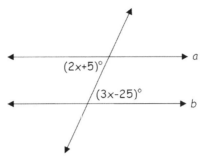

    a. x = 22
    b. x = 30
    c. x = 40
    d. *x* = 65

12. $\overrightarrow{DB}$ is a perpendicular bisector of $\overline{AC}$. If $AB = 4x-6$, $CB = 2x + 2$, and $DB = 6$, what is the length of $\overline{AC}$?

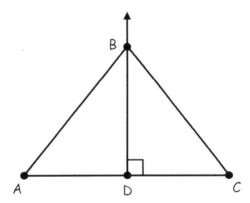

    a. 4
    b. 8
    c. 10
    d. 16

13. Examine the figure below. What is the measure of ∠C?

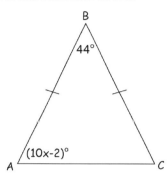

   a. 44°
   b. 68°
   c. 88°
   d. 136°

14. Based on the figure below, if $BG = 6x - 4$ and $GD = 2x + 8$, what is the length of $\overline{GD}$?

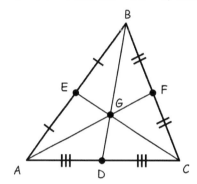

   a. 10
   b. 14
   c. 28
   d. 56

15. 15. In the figure shown below, *ABCD* is a parallelogram.

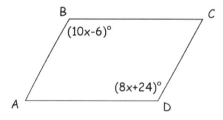

Find the measure of ∠ADC.

   a. 15°
   b. 56°
   c. 96°
   d. 144°

16. The following four steps are needed to bisect a line segment using a compass and straightedge. However, the steps are out of order. Using the numbers listed before each step, identify the correct order of steps for bisecting a line segment.

1 – Without changing the compass width again, set the compass point on the other segment endpoint and draw arcs above and below the segment so that they intersect the previous arcs.

2 – Draw a line segment. Place a compass point on one end of the segment and extend the compass width to be over half of the segment.

3 – Using a straightedge, draw a line between the points where the arcs intersected, which will bisect the line segment.

4 – Without changing the compass width, draw arcs above and below the segment.

    a. 1, 3, 2, 4
    b. 3, 2, 4, 1
    c. 2, 4, 1, 3
    d. 4, 1, 3, 2

17. Examine the following steps:

Step 1 – Using a compass, draw a circle.

Step 2 – Keeping the radius of the compass fixed, mark a point on the circle.

Step 3 – Centered at that point, draw an arc across the circle and mark a point at that intersection.

Step 4 – Center the compass at that new point, draw another arc across the circle and mark that point.

Step 5 – Continue drawing arcs along the circle until there are six points.

Step 6 – Using a straightedge, connect every other point.

The previous steps describe the construction of which shape inscribed in a circle?

    a. Equilateral Triangle
    b. Regular Hexagon
    c. Regular Pentagon
    d. Square

18. If rectangle $ABCD$ is dilated by a scale factor of $\frac{1}{2}$ to create its image $A'B'C'D'$, how does the slope of $\overleftrightarrow{AC}$ compare to the slope of $\overleftrightarrow{A'C'}$?

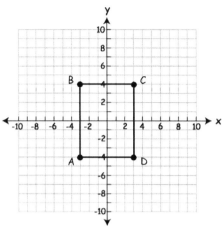

    a. The slope of $\overleftrightarrow{A'C'}$ is half the slope of $\overleftrightarrow{AC}$.
    b. The slope of $\overleftrightarrow{A'C'}$ is double the slope of $\overleftrightarrow{AC}$.
    c. The slope of $\overleftrightarrow{A'C'}$ is the same as the slope of $\overleftrightarrow{AC}$.
    d. The slope of $\overleftrightarrow{A'C'}$ is the reciprocal of the slope of $\overleftrightarrow{AC}$.

19. If $\overline{PQ}$, shown below, is dilated by a scale factor of 4, what are the new coordinates of Q'?

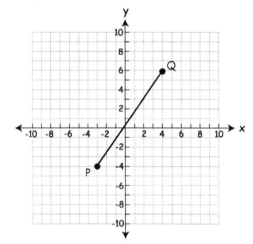

    a. (16, 24)
    b. (8, 10)
    c. (1, 1.5)
    d. (0, 2)

20. Which pair of figures below is similar?

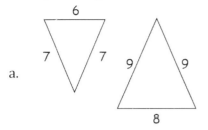

a.

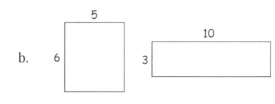

b.

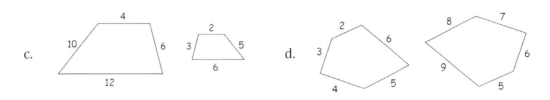

c.

d.

21. Examine the triangles below.

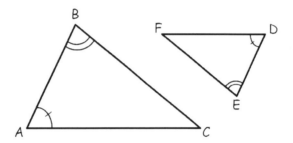

Which of the following theorems can be used to prove that $\triangle ABC \sim \triangle DEF$?

a. AA
b. ASA
c. SAS
d. SSS

22. Given the figure below and that $a = 6$ and $b = 8$, solve for the values x and h.

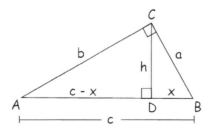

a. $x = 3.6$ and h $= 4.8$
b. x $= 4.8$ and h $= 5.2$
c. x $= 2.4$ and h $= 3.2$
d. x $= 10$ and $h = 3.2$

23. In the figure below, $\triangle ABC \cong \triangle DEF$.

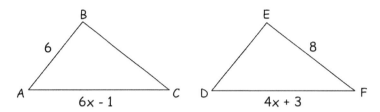

Find the perimeter of $\triangle DEF$.

    a. 16
    b. 19
    c. 21
    d. 25

24. In $\triangle ABC$, $\cos A =$

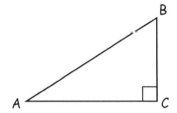

    a. $\dfrac{AC}{AB}$
    b. $\dfrac{AC}{BC}$
    c. $\dfrac{BC}{AC}$
    d. $\dfrac{BC}{AB}$

25. Sin 38° is equivalent to which of the following values?

    a. sin 142°
    b. sin 52°
    c. cos 52°
    d. cos 38°

26. A 600 m tall radio tower uses 720 m long guide wires for support, as shown in the figure below.

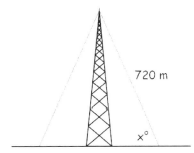

720 m

x°

What is the measure of the angle between the ground and the guide wire, as denoted by *x*?

    a. 33.6°
    b. 39.8°
    c. 50.2°
    d. 56.4°

27. A bird sits on top of a 15 ft tall lamp post. Looking down at a 35° angle of depression, the bird sees a bug on the ground. How far is the bug from the base of the lamp post?

    a. 10.5 ft
    b. 18.3 ft
    c. 21.4 ft
    d. 26.2 ft

28. Which of the following formulas can be used to find the area of the triangle shown below?

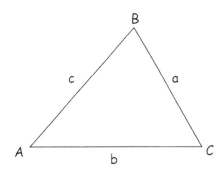

    a. $A = \frac{1}{2} ab \sin(C)$
    b. $A = \frac{1}{2} ab \sin(B)$
    c. $A = \frac{1}{2} bc \sin(B)$
    d. $A = \frac{1}{2} ac \sin(C)$

29. Based on Δ*ABC* below, what is the value of *x*?

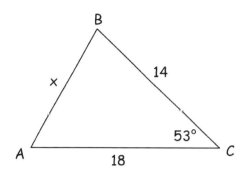

    a. 10.8
    b. 11.3
    c. 14.7
    d. 22.8

30. Sidney and Robert drive to school each school day. The following map shows the locations of Sidney's house and Robert's house in relation to the school.

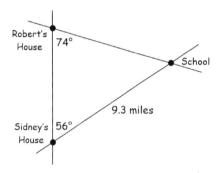

Based on the information in the map, how far does Robert have to drive to get to school in the morning?

    a. 7.0 miles
    b. 8.0 miles
    c. 10.8 miles
    d. 18.9 miles

31. Which of the following ratios can be used to prove that all circles are similar?

    a. $\dfrac{\text{Area}}{\text{Circumference}}$

    b. $\dfrac{\text{Circumference}}{\text{Diameter}}$

    c. $\dfrac{\text{Radius}}{\text{Area}}$

    d. $\dfrac{\text{Area}}{\text{Radius}}$

32. $\overline{AB}$ is tangent to Circle O. Find the length of $\overline{OB}$.

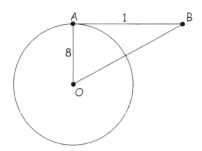

    a. 13
    b. 16
    c. 17
    d. 23

33. Quadrilateral *ABCD* is inscribed in Circle O.

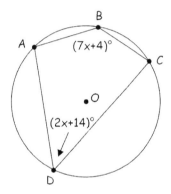

What is the measure of $\angle ADC$?
    a. 18°
    b. 30°
    c. 50°
    d. 90°

34. The sides of quadrilateral *PQRS* are tangent to the circle. What is the perimeter of quadrilateral *PQRS*?

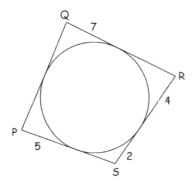

    a. 36
    b. 30
    c. 24
    d. 18

35. Examine Circle Q below.

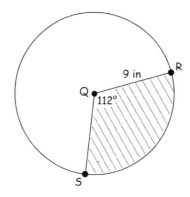

What is the area of sector QRS?

    a. 17.6 in²
    b. 79.2 in²
    c. 254.5 in²
    d. 316.7 in²

36. A circle is centered at (−5, 3) with a radius of 4. Which of the following equations describes that circle?

    a. $(x - 5)^2 + (y + 3)^2 = 4$
    b. $(x + 5)^2 + (y - 3)^2 = 4$
    c. $(x - 5)^2 + (y + 3)^2 = 16$
    d. $(x + 5)^2 + (y - 3)^2 = 16$

37. Which of the following equations represents a parabola with focus (2, 3) and directrix $y = -1$?

    a. $(y - 1)^2 = 8(x - 2)$
    b. $(y - 3)^2 = -4(x - 2)$
    c. $(x - 2)^2 = 8(y - 1)$
    d. $(x - 2)^2 = -4(y - 3)$

38. Which of the following equations represents an ellipse with foci (–2, 3) and (4, 3) and the sum of the distances from the foci to a point on the ellipse is 8?

    a. $\dfrac{(x-1)^2}{7} + \dfrac{(y-3)^2}{16} = 1$
    b. $\dfrac{(x-1)^2}{16} + \dfrac{(y-3)^2}{7} = 1$
    c. $\dfrac{(x-1)^2}{55} + \dfrac{(y-3)^2}{64} = 1$
    d. $\dfrac{(x-1)^2}{64} + \dfrac{(y-3)^2}{55} = 1$

39. A circle centered at (3, 0) passes through the point (7, 0). Which of the following points also lies on the circle?

    a. $(0, 5)$
    b. $(1, 2\sqrt{5})$
    c. $(2, \sqrt{17})$
    d. $(6, \sqrt{7})$

40. Given the line $y = \dfrac{2}{3}x + 4$, find the equation of a line perpendicular to that line and that passes through the point (6, 2).

    a. $y = \dfrac{2}{3}x - 2$
    b. $y = -\dfrac{2}{3}x + 6$
    c. $y = \dfrac{3}{2}x - 7$
    d. $y = -\dfrac{3}{2}x + 11$

41. Given points A and B on a number line, where $A = -3$ and $B = 7$, find point C, located between A and B, such that C is four times farther from A than it is from B.

    a. –1
    b. 1
    c. 3
    d. 5

42. On a coordinate grid, rectangle $ABCD$ has the following coordinates: $A(-2, 7)$, $B(5, 7)$, $C(5, -1)$, and $D(-2, -1)$. What is the area of rectangle $ABCD$?

    a. 18 units^2
    b. 20 units^2
    c. 30 units^2
    d. 56 units^2

43. Which method listed below uses a regular polygon inscribed in a circle to derive the formula for the area of a circle?

    a. Dissection Argument
    b. Informal Limits Argument
    c. Inscribed Angle Theorem
    d. Pythagorean Theorem

44. In a comparison of two spheres, it is determined that all corresponding cross sections of the spheres have the same area. Based on Cavalieri's principle, what can be said about these two spheres?

    a. They have the same mass.
    b. They have the same volume.
    c. They have the same weight.
    d. They have the same density.

45. A farmer installed a new grain silo on his property in preparation for the fall harvest. If the silo is in the shape of a cylinder with a diameter of 8 m and a height of 24 m, how much grain will the farmer be able to store in the silo?

    a. 402.1 m³
    b. 1,206.4 m³
    c. 1,608.5 m³
    d. 4,825.5 m³

46. Jack works at an ice cream shop. While placing an order, a customer asked for a sugar cone to be filled in completely level with ice cream before adding any scoops of ice cream on top. If the sugar cone has a diameter of 5 cm and it is 12.5 cm tall, how much ice cream will Jack use to fill the inside of the sugar cone?

    a. 81.8 cm3
    b. 245.4 cm3
    c. 327.2 cm3
    d. 981.7 cm³

47. If a horizontal cross-section was taken of the following triangular prism, what would be the resulting two-dimensional shape?

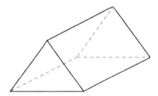

    a. Rectangle
    b. Trapezoid
    c. Triangle
    d. Square

48. The Great Pyramid of Khufu, located in Egypt, is the largest pyramid in the world. In the shape of a square pyramid, the Great Pyramid of Khufu has a height of 481 ft and the length of each side of the base is 756 ft. What is the volume of the Great Pyramid of Khufu?

  a. 1.21×105 ft³
  b. 4.85×105 ft³
  c. 9.16×107 ft³
  d. 2.75×10^8 ft³

49. The city of Minneapolis, Minnesota covers 54.9 square miles of land and has a population of 382,578. What is the population density of Minneapolis?

  a. 126.9 persons/square mile
  b. 6,968.6 persons/square mile
  c. 4,533,532.2 persons/square mile
  d. 248,890,917.9 persons/square mile

50. Zack is building a sand box for his children. A local home improvement store sells bags of sand for \$3.75/bag and each bag contains 0.5 cubic feet of sand. If the sand box has the dimensions 6 ft × 4 ft × 1 ft, how much will it cost Zack to completely fill the sand box with sand?

  a. \$24
  b. \$45
  c. \$90
  d. \$180

Answers and Explanations

Math.Content.G.CO.1

1. B: Parallel lines are two distinct lines in the same plane that do not intersect. Answer A is the definition of perpendicular lines. Answer C is the definition of opposite rays, which form a line. Answer D is the definition of an angle.

Math.Content.G.CO.2

2. D: A transformation is described as a function that takes points in the plane as inputs and gives other points as outputs. In Answer A, coincident means that two images are superimposed on one another. In Answer B, invariant means a property that cannot be changed by a given transformation. In Answer C, mensuration is the measurement of geometric figures, such as length, area, angle measure and volume.

Math.Content.G.CO.3

3. A: A 180° clockwise rotation about the origin takes the original coordinates and negates them. Therefore, the original coordinates of (x, y) become $(-x, -y)$ after the rotation. Answer B is the coordinate change after a 90° clockwise rotation about the origin. Answer C is the coordinate change after a 90° counterclockwise rotation about the origin. Answer D is the Answer B is the coordinate change after a reflection across the line $y = x$.

Math.Content.G.CO.3

4. C: A reflection is a transformation producing a mirror image. A figure reflected over the x-axis will have its vertices in the form (x, y) transformed to $(x, -y)$. The point W at (1,-7) reflects to W' at (1,7). Only Answer C shows $WXYZ$ being carried onto its image $W'X'Y'Z'$ by a reflection across the x-axis. Answer A shows a reflection across the line $y = x$. Answer B shows a 90° counterclockwise rotation about the origin. Answer D shows a reflection across the y-axis.

Math.Content.G.CO.4

5. D: For a reflection across the line $y = x$, the original coordinate points of (x, y) reverse to become (y, x) for the image. Therefore, since T is located at $(7, -4)$, the coordinates of T' after the reflection across the line $y = x$ become $(-4, 7)$. Answer A is for a reflection across the x-axis. Answer B is for a reflection across the y-axis. Answer C is for a 90° clockwise rotation about the origin.

Math.Content.G.CO.5

6. C: Since $EFGH$ is initially located in Quadrant II, a 90° clockwise rotation will rotate the image into Quadrant I. As $EFGH$ is rotated 90° clockwise, each vertex of the figure will undergo the coordinate transition of $(x, y) \rightarrow (y, -x)$, as is the case in Answer C. Answer A is a reflection across the y-axis. Answer B is a reflection across the x-axis. Answer D is a 90° counterclockwise rotation.

Math.Content.G.CO.5

7. B: To determine the translation, compare the coordinates of $J(-4, 1)$ and $J'(2, -7)$. To find the change in the x-direction, subtract the x coordinate of the starting position from the final position that is $\Delta x = 2 - (-4) = 2 + 4 = 6$. Similarly, the change in the y-direction is $-7 - 1 = -8$. We can check that the same is true for the other vertices. Therefore, the rule that describes the translation of $JKLM$ to its image $J'K'L'M'$ is $(x, y) \rightarrow (x + 6, y - 8)$. Answer A incorrectly used the opposite signs. Answer C incorrectly used the opposite signs and had the *x* and *y* directions reversed. Answer D had the *x* and *y* directions reversed.

Math.Content.G.CO.6

8. A: In order for two figures to be congruent, they must have the same size and shape. The two triangles in Answer A have the same size and shape, even though the second triangle is rotated counterclockwise compared to the first triangle. The rectangles in Answer B are the same shape, but they are not the same size. In Answer C, the second circle has been vertically stretched, so the figures are not the same shape or size. In Answer D, the second trapezoid has been horizontally stretched so it is not the same size as the first trapezoid.

Math.Content.G.CO.7

9. D: Since the two triangles have all three corresponding pairs of sides and corresponding pairs of angles marked congruent, then the two triangles are congruent. Similar triangles are the same shape but not necessarily the same size; they have congruent angles. All congruent triangles are similar triangles, so Answer D is the best choice. In Answer C, equilateral triangles are triangles that have sides with all the same measure within the same triangle, not in relation to another triangle.

Math.Content.G.CO.8

10. A: In order for triangles to be congruent by ASA, there needs to be two pairs of congruent corresponding angles and then the pair of sides between those angles is also congruent. The triangles in Answer A meet the requirements for ASA triangle congruence. In Answer B, the triangles are congruent by AAS. In Answer C, the triangles are congruent by SAS. In Answer D, the triangles are congruent by HL (Hypotenuse Leg).

Math.Content.G.CO.9

11. B: The listed angles are located in the alternate interior angles position. According to the Alternate Interior Angle Theorem, when a transversal cuts across parallel lines, the alternate interior angles are congruent. Since lines *a* and *b* are parallel, it means that $2x + 5 = 3x - 25$. After subtracting $2x$ from both sides and adding 25 to both sides, the equation simplifies as $30 = x$. In Answer A, the angles were incorrectly treated as complementary. In Answer C, the angles were incorrectly treated as supplementary. Answer D is the measure of each alternate interior angle, but the question only wanted the value of *x*.

Math.Content.G.CO.9

12. D: The Perpendicular Bisector Theorem states that the points on a perpendicular bisector of a line segment are exactly those equidistant from the segment's endpoints. Since the point B lies on $\overrightarrow{DB}$, the perpendicular bisector of $\overline{AC}$, it means that the point B is equidistant from both *A* and *C*, giving us $AB = CB$. Therefore, $4x - 6 = 2x + 2$. After subtracting $2x$ from both sides and adding 6 to both sides, the equation simplifies as $2x = 8$. Divide both sides by 2 to get $x = 4$. Substituting for *x*, $AB = 4(4) - 6 = 16 - 6 = 10$ and $CB = 2(4) + 2 = 10$. The question asks for the length of $\overline{AC}$, which is the base of $\triangle ABC$. Since $\overrightarrow{DB}$ is a perpendicular bisector, it divides $\triangle ABC$ into two right triangles in which the length of $\overline{AD}$ equals the length of $\overline{DC}$. Since we know that $AB = 10$ and $DB = 6$, we can use the Pythagorean Theorem to find the length of $\overline{AD}$: $(AD)^2 + (DB)^2 = (AB)^2$, $(AD)^2 + 6^2 = 10^2$, $(AD)^2 + 36 = 100$. Subtract 36 from both sides to get $(AD)^2 = 64$. Take the square root of both sides to get

AD = 8. Since AD is half the length of AC, AC = 2(8) = 16. Answer A is the value of x. Answer B is the length for each $\overline{AD}$ and $\overline{DC}$. Answer C is the length for each $\overline{AB}$ and $\overline{CB}$.

Math.Content.G.CO.10

13. B: According to the Triangle Sum Theorem, the measures of the three angles in a triangle sum to 180°. Therefore, in the triangle shown, $m\angle A + m\angle B + m\angle C = 180°$. However, we are not initially given the measure of $\angle C$. But, since the triangle is isosceles, the Isosceles Triangle Theorem states that in an isosceles triangle, the base angles (or angles opposite the congruent sides) are congruent. So, in this triangle, $m\angle A = m\angle C$. By substitution, the angle measure equation becomes $10x - 2 + 44 + 10x - 2 = 180$. Simplifying the left side of the equation becomes $20x + 40 = 180$. After subtracting 40 from both sides, the equation becomes $20x = 140$. Finally, divide both sides by 20 to get $x = 7$. Then, substitute that value for x into the expression for the measure of $\angle C$: 10(7) – 2 = 70 – 2 = 68°. Answer A incorrectly assumed that the $\angle B$ and $\angle C$ were the congruent angles in the isosceles triangle. Answer C incorrectly doubled the measure of $\angle B$. Answer D incorrectly set up the equation as $10x - 2 + 44 = 180$ to get the angle measure of 136°.

Math.Content.G.CO.10

14. C: In ΔABC, the midpoints are marked as D, E, and F. The medians of the triangle are then drawn in as $\overline{AF}$, $\overline{BD}$ and $\overline{CE}$. The medians intersect at a point called the centroid. Based on this intersection, it is the case that AG = 2GF, BG = 2GD, and CG = 2GE. Since we are given that BG = 6x– 4 and GD = 2x + 8, we can set up the equation as 6x – 4 = 2(2x + 8). Simplifying that equation, it becomes 6x – 4 = 4x + 16. After subtracting 4x from both sides and adding 4 to both sides, the equation becomes 2x = 20. Divide both sides by 2 to get x = 10. Then, the length of $\overline{GD}$ is calculated as 2(10) + 8 = 20 + 8 = 28. Answer A is the value of x. Answer B is the length of $\overline{GD}$ if the equation was incorrectly set up as BG = GD. Answer D is the length of $\overline{BG}$.

Math.Content.G.CO.11

15. D: One of the theorems about parallelograms states that the opposite angles in a parallelogram are congruent. Therefore, according to the figure, $\angle ABC \cong \angle ADC$, so $m\angle ABC = m\angle ADC$. By substitution, that equation becomes $10x - 6 = 8x + 14$. After subtracting 8x from both sides and adding 6 to both sides, the equation simplifies as 2x = 30. Divide both sides by 2 to get x = 15. To find the measure of $\angle ADC$, substitute the value for x into the expression for $\angle ADC$: 8(15) + 24 = 120 + 24 = 144°. Answer A is just the value of x. Answer B is the measure of $\angle ADC$ if the angles were incorrectly thought to be complementary angles. Answer C is the measure of $\angle ADC$ is the angles were incorrectly thought to be supplementary angles.

Math.Content.G.CO.12

16. C: The correct sequence of steps for bisecting a line segment is 2, 4, 1, 3.

Math.Content.G.CO.13

17. A: The listed steps describe the construction of an equilateral triangle inscribed in a circle. If every point was connected using a straightedge, that would have constructed a regular hexagon instead.

Math.Content.G.SRT.1a

18. C: Since rectangle $ABCD$ is centered at the origin and $\overleftrightarrow{AC}$ passes through the origin, any dilation of rectangle $ABCD$ will leave that line unchanged. Since A has the coordinates $(-3 -4)$ and C has the coordinates $(3, 4)$, the slope of $\overleftrightarrow{AC} = \frac{4-(-4)}{3-(-3)} = \frac{8}{6} = \frac{4}{3}$. When rectangle $ABCD$ is dilated by a scale factor of $\frac{1}{2}$ to create image $A'B'C'D'$, A' has the coordinates $(-1.5, -2)$ and C' has the coordinates $(1.5, 2)$. The slope of $\overleftrightarrow{A'C'} = \frac{2-(-2)}{1.5-(-1.5)} = \frac{4}{3}$. Therefore, the slope of $\overleftrightarrow{A'C'}$ is the same as the slope of $\overleftrightarrow{AC}$.

Math.Content.G.SRT.1b

19. A: If $\overline{PQ}$ is dilated by a scale factor of 4, then the coordinates of P and Q are each multiplied by 4. For point Q, $(4, 6)$ then becomes $(16, 24)$ to get Q'. Answer B results if 4 were added to the coordinates. Answer C results if the coordinates were divided by 4. Answer D results if 4 were subtracted from the coordinates.

Math.Content.G.SRT.2

20. C: In order for figures to be similar, all sets of corresponding sides need to be proportional. All corresponding sides in Answer C are at a 2:1 ratio. In Answer A, the corresponding sides are 2 more for the second figure, instead of being 2 times larger. In Answer B, one set of corresponding sides is at a 1:2 ratio, while the other set of corresponding sides is at a 2:1 ratio. In Answer D, the corresponding sides are 3 more for the second figure, instead of being 3 times larger.

Math.Content.G.SRT.3

21. A: Given the measure of two angles of a triangle, we can find the measure of the remaining angle by the relationship $m\angle BCA = 180° - (m\angle ABC + m\angle CAB)$. Since each triangle shows two pairs of congruent corresponding angles, we know the third pair of angles must be congruent as well. Since all 3 pairs of corresponding angles are congruent, $\triangle ABC$ is similar to $\triangle DEF$. This is known as the AA Similarity Theorem.

Math.Content.G.SRT.4

22. A: Noticing that $\angle BCD$ and $\angle CAD$ are both complimentary to $\angle ACD$, we have that $m\angle BCD = m\angle CAD = m\angle CAB$. By Angle Angle similarity, we know these are similar triangles. By the Pythagorean theorem, $c = \sqrt{a^2 + b^2} = \sqrt{6^2 + 8^2} = 10$. Because ACB is similar to CBD, we have the ratio $\frac{h}{a} = \frac{b}{c}$. Solving for h yields $h = \frac{ab}{c} = \frac{6*8}{10} = 4.8$. Similarly, consider the ratio $\frac{x}{a} = \frac{a}{c}$ and solve for x, giving $x = \frac{a^2}{c} = \frac{(6)^2}{10} = 3.6$.

Math.Content.G.SRT.5

23. D: In order to find the perimeter of $\triangle DEF$, we need to know the values of all three sides of the triangle. We are given that $EF = 8$. Since $\triangle ABC \cong \triangle DEF$, then $DE = AB$, which means that $DE = 6$ as well. Also, since $\triangle ABC \cong \triangle DEF$, then $AC = DF$. Therefore, $6x - 1 = 4x + 3$. After subtracting $4x$ from both sides and adding 1 to both sides, the equation becomes $2x = 4$. Divide both sides by 2 to get $x = 2$. After substituting for x, the value of DF becomes $4(2) + 3 = 8 + 3 = 11$. The perimeter of $\triangle DEF$ then becomes $6 + 8 + 11 = 25$. In Answer A, after solving for x, the value of 2 was incorrectly used for the length of $\overline{DF}$ instead of substituting that value into the $4x + 3$ expression to get the side length. In Answer B, only the sides 8 and 11 were added. In Answer C, after setting up the equation as $6x - 1 = 4x + 3$, although $4x$ was correctly subtracted from both sides, 1 was incorrectly subtracted instead of added to both sides and the equation was incorrectly simplified as $2x = 2$ which results in $x = 1$. Then, $4(1) + 3 = 7$.which leads to an incorrect perimeter of $6 + 8 + 7 = 21$.

Math.Content.G.SRT.6

24. A: The cosine function is represented by the ratio $\frac{adjacent\ leg}{hypotenuse}$. In $\triangle ABC$, the adjacent leg to $\angle A$ is AC and the hypotenuse is AB. Therefore, $\cos A = \frac{AC}{AB}$. Answer B is $\cot A$. Answer C is $\tan A$. Answer D is $\sin A$.

Math.Content.G.SRT.7

25. C: The sine of one angle is equivalent to the cosine of the complementary angle. Therefore, since $90° - 38° = 52°$, then $\sin 38° = \cos 52°$. In Answer A, $142°$ is the supplementary angle to $38°$, but it needs to be the complementary angle. Answer B is the complementary angle, but it is in terms of sine instead of cosine. Answer D is the cosine but the same angle instead of the complementary angle.

Math.Content.G.SRT.8

26. D: The radio tower, the guide wire, and the ground form a right triangle. The guide wire forms the hypotenuse and the radio tower forms the leg opposite of angle x. Therefore, in order to solve for the measure of angle x, it needs to be set up as $\sin x = \frac{opposite\ leg}{hypotenuse}$ or $\sin x = \frac{600}{720}$. The value of x is found using the calculation $x = \sin^{-1}\left(\frac{600}{720}\right) = 56.4°$. Answer A incorrectly used $\cos x = \frac{600}{720}$. Answer B incorrectly used $\tan x = \frac{600}{720}$. Answer C incorrectly used $\tan x = \frac{720}{600}$.

Math.Content.G.SRT.8

27. C: Since there was no figure provided with the problem, a figure should be drawn and labeled as follows:

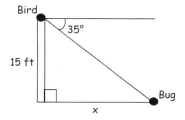

The sight line of the bird looking straight ahead is parallel to the ground, so the 35° angle of depression is congruent to the angle of elevation due to the Alternate Interior Angle Theorem. Therefore, the focus of the problem becomes a right triangle labeled as follows:

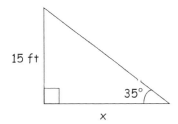

Since the legs opposite and adjacent to the 35° angle are labeled, the equation is set up as $\tan 35° = \frac{15}{x}$. Solving for x, the equation becomes $x = \frac{15}{\tan 35°} = 21.4$ ft. In Answer A, the equation was incorrectly set up as $\tan 35° = \frac{x}{15}$. In Answer B, the equation was incorrectly set up as $\cos 35° = \frac{15}{x}$. In Answer D, the equation was incorrectly set up as $\sin 35° = \frac{15}{x}$.

Math.Content.G.SRT.9

28. A: The general formula for a triangle is $A = \frac{1}{2} \times base \times height$. In this triangle, the base is length b. For the height of the triangle, draw in an altitude from vertex B perpendicular to side $\overline{AC}$. Then, $\sin C = \frac{height}{a}$. Solving that equation for the height yields $height = a \sin(C)$. Therefore, the formula for the area of a triangle becomes $A = \frac{1}{2} \times b \times a \sin(C)$, which can be rearranged as $A = \frac{1}{2} ab \sin(C)$.

Math.Content.G.SRT.10

29. C: In the figure, since the given angle is located between the two given sides, we need to use the Law of Cosines to solve for x. The Law of Cosines is $c^2 = a^2 + b^2 - 2ab \cos(C)$. If we let $a = 14$, $b = 18$ and $c = x$, then the Law of Cosines becomes $x^2 = 14^2 + 18^2 - 2(14)(18) \cos(53°)$.. This simplifies as $x^2 = 216.69$.. Therefore, $x = 14.7$. Answer A used sine instead of cosine in the formula. Answer B incorrectly used the Pythagorean Theorem with $x^2 + 14^2 = 18^2$, instead of using the Law of Cosines. Answer D also incorrectly used the Pythagorean Theorem with $14^2 + 18^2 = x^2$.

Math.Content.G.SRT.11

30. B: Since the map shows a triangle with a 74° angle, the length of the side opposite the 74° angle, a 56° angle, and it asks for length of the side opposite of the 56° angle (which we will call x), the Law of Sines is needed to find the missing side length. The Law of Sines is $\frac{\sin A}{a} = \frac{\sin B}{b} = \frac{\sin C}{c}$, but to solve this problem we only need $\frac{\sin A}{a} = \frac{\sin B}{b}$. By substitution, that equation becomes $\frac{\sin 74°}{9.3} = \frac{\sin 56°}{x}$. Solving for x, the equation results in $x = \frac{9.3 \sin 56°}{\sin 74°} = 8.0$ miles. In Answer A, the equation was incorrectly set up as just $\frac{74}{9.3} = \frac{56}{x}$. In Answer C, the equation was incorrectly set up as $9.3 \sin 74° = x \sin 56°$. Answer D is the length of x if the equation was incorrectly set up as $\frac{\cos A}{a} = \frac{\cos B}{b}$.

Math.Content.G.C.1

31. B: In all circles, the formula for the circumference of the circle is $Circumferece = \pi \times Diameter$. If we rearrange that equation, it becomes $\frac{Circumference}{Diameter} = \pi$. Therefore, in any circle, the ratio of the circumference to the diameter is always equal to π. As a result, all circles are similar.

Math.Content.G.C.2

32. C: Since $\overline{AB}$ is tangent to Circle O, then $\overline{AB}$ forms a right angle with radius $A\overset{\frown}{O}$. ΔAUB is then a right triangle, so the Pythagorean Theorem can be used to find the measure of $\overline{OB}$. Therefore, $(OB)^2 = 8^2 + 15^2 = 64 + 225 =, 289$. After taking the square root of both sides, it becomes $17 = OB$.

Math.Content.G.C.3

33. C: If a quadrilateral is inscribed in a circle, then its opposite angles are supplementary. Therefore, $m\angle ABC + m\angle ADC = 180°$. By substitution, that equation becomes $7x + 4 + 2x + 14 = 180$. The equation simplifies as $9x + 18 = 180$. After subtracting 18 from both sides, the equation becomes $9x = 162$. Divide both sides by 9 to get $x = 18$. Substituting for x in the expression results in $2(18) + 14 = 36 + 14 = 50°$. Answer A is the value of x. Answer B is the measure of $\angle ADC$ if $\angle ABC$ and $\angle ADC$ were incorrectly thought to be complementary instead of supplementary. Answer D is the measure if the equation was incorrectly set up as $m\angle ABC + m\angle ADC = 360°$, but 360° is the measure of all four angles.

Math.Content.G.C.4

34. A: For any point outside a circle, there are exactly two lines tangent to the circle passing through that point. Further, the lengths of these line segments from the point to the circle are equal. In this problem, the two segments extending from Q both have a length of 7. The two segments extending from R have a length of 4. The two segments extending from S have a length of 2. The two segments extending from P have a length of 5. Therefore, the perimeter of quadrilateral $PQRS$ can be calculated at $7 + 7 + 4 + 4 + 2 + 2 + 5 + 5 = 36$.

Math.Content.G.C.5

35. B: The area of the sector of a circle is calculated using the equation: $\frac{Central\ Angle\ Measure}{360°} \times \pi r^2$, where r is the radius of the circle. Since the central angle measure is 112° and the radius is 9 in, the equation becomes: $\frac{112°}{360°} \times \pi (9\ in)^2 = 79.2\ in^2$. Answer A found the length of the arc intercepted by $\angle RQS$. Answer C is the area of the circle. Answer D used the diameter length instead of the radius in the calculation.

Math.Content.G.GPE.1

36. D: The equation for a circle is $(x - h)^2 + (y - k)^2 = r^2$, where (h, k) is the center of the circle and r is the radius. Since the center of the circle is (−5, 3) and the radius is 4, those values can be substituted into the equation as $\left(x - (-5)\right)^2 + (y - 3)^2 = 4^2$ which simplifies as $(x + 5)^2 + (y - 3)^2 = 16$. Answers A and B did not square the radius. Answers A and C did not subtract the center values from x and y when they were substituted into the equation.

Math.Content.G.GPE.2

37. C: Since the focus is at $(2, 3)$ and the directrix is the line $y = -1$, the vertex of the parabola is halfway between those values. Therefore, the vertex is located at $(2, 1)$. Since the focus is located above the vertex, the parabola opens up. A parabola that opens up has the general equation of $(x - h)^2 = 4p(y - k)$, where (h, k) is the vertex and the absolute value of p is the distance between the focus and the vertex and the distance between the vertex and directrix. In this problem, the focus is $(2, 3)$ and the vertex is $(2, 1)$, so $|p| = |(3 - 1)| = |2| = 2$. Since the focus is above the vertex, the value of p is positive, so $p = 2$. Substituting the values for the vertex and p into the equation, it becomes: $(x - 2)^2 = 4(2)(y - 1)$ and simplifies as $(x - 2)^2 = 8(y - 1)$. Answer A incorrectly set up the equation as $(y - k)^2 = 4p(x - h)$. Answer B incorrectly set up the equation as $(y - k)^2 = 4p(x - h)$ and then incorrectly used the focus for (h, k) and the directrix for p. Answer D correctly used the equation of $(x - h)^2 = 4p(y - k)$, but then incorrectly used the focus for (h, k) and the directrix for p.

Math.Content.G.GPE.3

38. B: Since the foci are located along the line $y = 3$, the major axis of the ellipse is horizontal. This means the general equation for the ellipse is $\frac{(x-h)^2}{a^2} + \frac{(y-k)^2}{b^2} = 1$, where (h, k) is the center of the ellipse, a is half the length of the major axis and b is half the length of the minor axis. Since the center is located between the foci of $(-2, 3)$ and $(4, 3)$, the center of the ellipse is located at $(1, 3)$ and the distance from the center to each focus, c, is 3. The sum of the distances from the foci to a point on the ellipse is equivalent to $2a$. Therefore, $2a = 8$, so $a = 4$ and $a^2 = 16$. To find the value of b^2, we use the equation $b^2 = a^2 - c^2$. Substituting in for that equation, $b^2 = 4^2 - 3^2 = 16 - 9 = 7$. Based on the center $(1, 3)$ and the squares of the axes $a^2 = 16$ and $b^2 = 7$, the equation for the ellipse becomes $\frac{(x-1)^2}{16} + \frac{(y-3)^2}{7} = 1$. Answer A incorrectly set up the equation as $\frac{(x-h)^2}{b^2} + \frac{(y-k)^2}{a^2} = 1$. Answer C incorrectly set up the equation as $\frac{(x-h)^2}{b^2} + \frac{(y-k)^2}{a^2} = 1$ and then incorrectly used $a = 8$, which made $a^2 = 64$ and $b^2 = 64 - 9 = 55$. Answer D incorrectly used $a = 8$, which made $a^2 = 64$ and $b^2 = 64 - 9 = 55$.

Math.Content.G.GPE.4

39. D: A circle centered at $(3, 0)$ that passes through the point $(7, 0)$ has a radius, r, of 4 units, since $r = \sqrt{(7-3)^2 + (0-0)^2} = \sqrt{(4)^2 + (0)^2} = \sqrt{16 + 0} = \sqrt{16} = 4$. The equation for a circle with a center of $(3, 0)$ and $r = 4$ is $(x - 3)^2 + (y - 0)^2 = 4^2$, which simplifies as $(x - 3)^2 + y^2 = 16$. Substituting in the points above into the circle equation, only Answer D correctly works since $(6 - 3)^2 + \left(\sqrt{7}\right)^2 = (3)^2 + \left(\sqrt{7}\right)^2 = 9 + 7 = 16$. Answer A results if $(0 - 3)^2$ is incorrectly simplified as -9. Answer B results if $(1 - 3)^2$ is incorrectly simplified as -4. Answer C results if $(2 - 3)^2$ is incorrectly simplified as -1.

Math.Content.G.GPE.5

40. D: The slope of the original line is $m = \frac{2}{3}$. Since the new line needs to be perpendicular, the new slope needs to be the negative reciprocal of the original slope. The negative reciprocal of $\frac{2}{3}$ is $-\frac{3}{2}$. The given point is $(6, 2)$, which is equivalent to (x_1, y_1) in the point-slope equation of $y - y_1 = m(x - x_1)$. Substituting in the new slope and given point, the point-slope equation becomes $y - 2 = -\frac{3}{2}(x - 6)$. Distributing on the right side of the equation results in $y - 2 = -\frac{3}{2}x + 9$. Add 2 to

- 91 -

both sides of the equation to get the perpendicular line of $y = -\frac{3}{2}x + 11$. Answer A found a parallel line. Answer B took the opposite slope instead of the opposite reciprocal slope. Answer C took the reciprocal slope instead of the opposite reciprocal slope.

Math.Content.G.GPE.6

41. D: If point C is four times farther from A than from B, it means that the ratio of distances from C to A and B is 4:1, respectively. Therefore, the line segment can be broken up into 4 + 1 = 5 equal segments. The total distance between points A and B is 7 – (–3) – 10 units. If we divide 10 by 5, each equal segment is 2 units in length. We can then multiply the ratio by 2 to get the actual distances of C from A and B, 4(2):1(2) = 8:2. So, C is located 8 units from A and 2 units from B. Since A is located at –3, it means that –3 + 8 = 5. Answer A is the location if C is four times farther from B than it is from A. Answer B is just four units from point A. Answer C is just four units from point B.

Math.Content.G.GPE.7

42. D: To find the area of rectangle $ABCD$, first start by plotting the rectangle on a coordinate grid, as shown below.

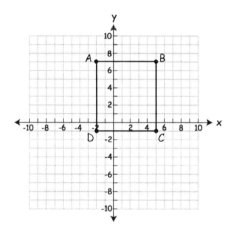

Then, since the sides of the rectangle are parallel to the x and y-axes, find the lengths of AB and BC. $AB = 5 -(-2) = 7$. $BC = 7 -(-1) = 8$. Therefore, the area of rectangle $ABCD$ is $(7)(8) = 56$ units^2. Answer A is the area if the length of the sides were incorrectly calculated as $AB = 5-2 = 3$ and $BC = 7-1 = 6$. Answer B is the area if the coordinate values were mixed up and the sides were incorrectly calculated as $AB = 5-1 = 4$ and $BC = 7-2=5$. Answer C is the perimeter of the rectangle.

Math.Content.G.GMD.1

43. B: It is the Informal Limits Argument that uses a regular polygon inscribed in a circle to derive the formula for the area of a circle. When a regular polygon is inscribed in a circle, the polygon can be broken up into many triangles with the vertex at the center of the circle and the base along the edge of the polygon. As the number of sides of the polygon is increased, the number of triangles is also increased. As the number of sides of the polygon gets larger, the combined area of each triangle within that polygon approaches the area of the circle. In Answer A, the Dissection Argument finds the area of a circle by breaking up the circle into wedges and then rearranging those wedges to form a rectangle. In Answer C, the Inscribed Angle Theorem states that the measure of an inscribed angle is half the measure of its intercepted arc. In Answer D, the

- 92 -

Pythagorean Theorem states that in a right triangle, the square of the hypotenuse is equal to the sum of the squares of the legs.

Math.Content.G.GMD.2

44. B: Based on Cavalieri's principle, if all corresponding cross sections of two solids have the same area, then those two solids also have the same volume.

Math.Content.G.GMD.3

45. B: The volume of the cylinder is the amount of grain that the farmer will be able to store in the silo. The formula for the volume of a cylinder is $V = \pi r^2 h$, where r is the radius and h is the height. Since the cylinder has a diameter of 8 m, the radius is half of the diameter, or 4 m. The height is 24 m. Therefore, by substitution, $V = \pi r^2 h$ becomes $V = \pi (4\ m)^2 (24\ m) = 1,206.4$ m³. Answer A used the volume formula for a cone. Answer C used the volume formula for a cone and the diameter of the cylinder. Answer D used the diameter instead of the radius in the volume formula.

Math.Content.G.GMD.3

46. A: The volume of the sugar cone is the amount of ice cream needed to completely fill in the sugar cone with ice cream. The formula for the volume of a cone is $V = \frac{1}{3}\pi r^2 h$, where r is the radius and h is the height of the cone. Since the cone has a diameter of 5 cm, the radius is half of the diameter, or 2.5 cm. The height of the cone is 12.5 cm. Therefore, by substitution, $V = \frac{1}{3}\pi r^2 h$ becomes $V = \frac{1}{3}\pi (2.5\ cm)^2 (12.5\ cm) = 81.8$ cm³. Answer B forgot to multiply by $\frac{1}{3}$. Answer C used the diameter instead of the radius in the formula. Answer D forgot to multiply by $\frac{1}{3}$ and used the diameter instead of the radius.

Math.Content.G.GMD.4

47. A: When a horizontal cross-section is taken of the triangular prism shown, the cross-section is parallel to the rectangular side along the ground. Therefore, the resulting two-dimensional shape is a rectangle. Answer C would be the result if a vertical cross-section was taken parallel to the triangle bases.

Math.Content.G.MG.1

48. C: The formula for the volume of a pyramid is $V = \frac{1}{3}BH$, where B is the area of the base and H is the height of the pyramid. Since the base is a square with a length of 756 ft on each side, the area of the base is A = s² = (756 ft)² = 571,536 ft². Therefore, with a base of 571,536 ft² and a height of 481 ft, the volume of the Great Pyramid of Khufu is $V = \frac{1}{3}(571,536\ ft^2)(481\ ft) = 9.16 \times 10^7$ ft³. Answer A just used the length of one side of the square for the base instead of the area of the base. Answer B used the perimeter of the base instead of the area. Answer D incorrectly used the formula $V = BH$.

Math.Content.G.MG.2

49. B: Population density is calculated by taking the population of a city and dividing that value by the square miles of land in the city. For Minneapolis, the population density is calculated as $\frac{382,578\ persons}{54.9\ square\ miles}$ = 6,968.6 persons/square mile. Answer A incorrectly calculated the population density by dividing 382,578 by 54.9². Answer C incorrectly multiplied the population by the land area. Answer D incorrectly multiplied the population by the 54.9².

Math.Content.G.MG.3

50. D: The cost for filling the sand box with sand is calculated by multiplying the cost/bag of sand by the number of bags needed. To determine the number of bags needed, first find the volume of the sand box: 6 ft× 4 ft× 1 ft = 24 cubic feet. Next, since each bag of sand contains 0.5 cubic feet of sand, the number of bags needed is $\frac{24 \; cubic \; feet}{0.5 \; cubic \; feet/bag}$ — 40 bags. Finally, since the cost/bag is $3.75, the cost for filling the sand box is $3.75/bag × 48 bags = $180. In Answer A, 24 is just the volume of the sand box. Answer B is the value if the number of bags of sand was incorrectly calculated by multiplying 24 × 0.5 instead of dividing 24÷0.5. Answer C is the value if the number of bags of sand was incorrectly thought to be the same as the volume of the box.

Practice Test #2

Practice Questions

1. "The set of all points that are a fixed distance from a given point" is the definition for which of the following terms?

    a. Angle
    b. Circle
    c. Line Segment
    d. Ray

2. Determine which of the following transformations preserves distance and angle.

a.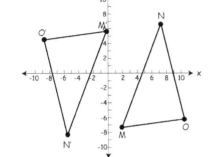

b.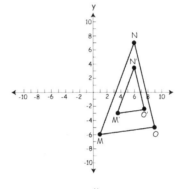

c.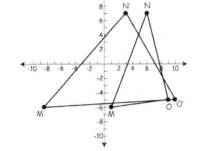

d.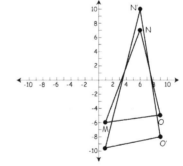

3. Based on the figure below, describe how rectangle **ABCD** can be carried onto its image **A'B'C'D'**.

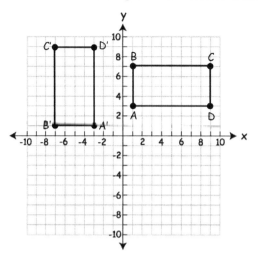

    a. Reflection across the x-axis
    b. Reflection across the y-axis
    c. Rotation 90° clockwise about the origin
    d. Rotation 90° counterclockwise about the origin

4. Examine the figure.

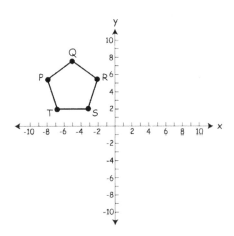

Identify the image $P'Q'R'S'T'$ that results if $PQRST$ is reflected across the line $y = x$.

a.

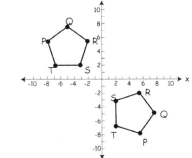

b.

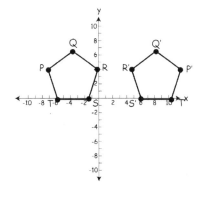

c.

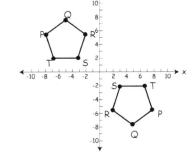

d.

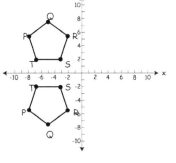

5. If $\overleftrightarrow{AB}$ was rotated 180° about the origin to form its image $\overleftrightarrow{A'B'}$, what type of lines would $\overleftrightarrow{AB}$ and $\overleftrightarrow{A'B'}$ create?

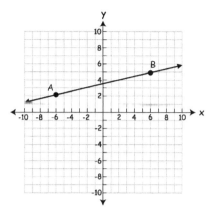

    a. Intersecting Lines
    b. Parallel Lines
    c. Perpendicular Lines
    d. Skew Lines

6. Which of the following terms is defined as "A transformation in which every point of a figure is moved the same distance and in the same direction to create the image"?
    a. Translation
    b. Rotation
    c. Reflection
    d. Dilation

7. Examine the figure below.

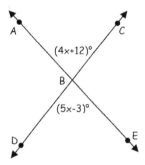

What is the measure of $\angle ABC$?

    a. 15°
    b. 48°
    c. 72°
    d. 88°

- 98 -

13. Lines p and q are parallel in the figure below. If $m\angle 3 = 8x + 24$ and $m\angle 7 = 10x - 6$, what is the measure of $\angle 4$?

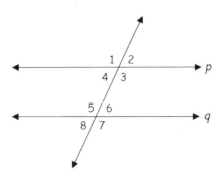

    a. 15°
    b. 36°
    c. 86°
    d. 144°

14. Find the measure of $\overline{BD}$ in the figure below.

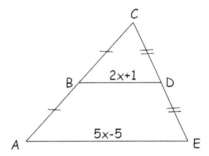

    a. 2
    b. 5
    c. 7
    d. 15

15. $JKLM$ is a parallelogram. If $JL = 13x - 11$ and $JN = 4x + 7$, what is the length of $\overline{JN}$.?

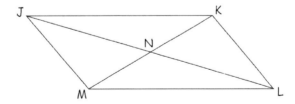

    a. 2
    b. 5
    c. 15
    d. 27

16. The statement "Without changing the compass width, place the compass on the new point, which is not on the segment, and then draw an arc in the area where the other endpoint will be located" is a necessary step in which of the following compass and straightedge constructions?

    a. Bisecting a line segment
    b. Copying a line segment
    c. Drawing parallel lines
    d. Drawing perpendicular lines

17. Which of the following steps is needed to construct a square inscribed in a circle?

    a. Without changing the compass width, place the compass on the new point, which is not on the segment, and then draw an arc in the area where the other endpoint will be located.
    b. Using a straightedge, draw a line from the angle vertex to the point where the two arcs intersect on the interior of the angle.
    c. Draw in the diameter of the circle and label the endpoints as B and C. Set your compass wider than it was to draw the circle and draw another circle, using B as the center.
    d. With the compass set to the same width as the radius, center the compass at a point on the circle and then draw an arc across the circle. Mark the point of intersection across the circle, then center the compass at the intersection point and repeat the steps to draw arcs around the circle.

18. If parallelogram **WXYZ**, shown below, is dilated by a scale factor of 3 to create image **W′X′Y′Z′**, what is the relationship between $\overleftrightarrow{WZ}$ and $\overleftrightarrow{W'Z'}$?

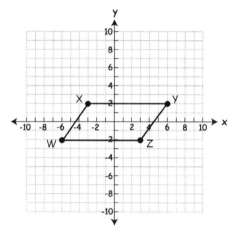

    a. $\overleftrightarrow{WZ}$ and $\overleftrightarrow{W'Z'}$ are parallel.
    b. $\overleftrightarrow{WZ}$ and $\overleftrightarrow{W'Z'}$ are perpendicular.
    c. $\overleftrightarrow{W'Z'}$ has a slope 3 times that of $\overleftrightarrow{WZ}$.
    d. $\overleftrightarrow{W'Z'}$ has a slope $\frac{1}{3}$ times that of $\overleftrightarrow{WZ}$.

- 100 -

19. In the figure below, ΔJKL is dilated to the image $\Delta J'K'L'$.

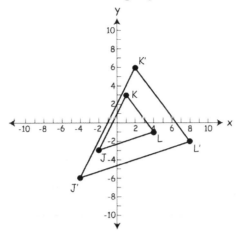

What is the scale factor of the dilation?

 a. $\frac{1}{3}$
 b. $\frac{1}{2}$
 c. 2
 d. 3

20. Examine the triangles below:

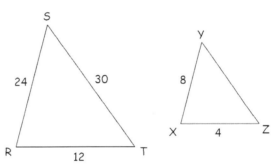

In order for ΔRST to be similar to ΔXYZ, what must be the length of $\overline{YZ}$?

 a. 10
 b. 14
 c. 15
 d. 22

21. Determine which of the following triangles can be proved similar by the AA Similarity Theorem.

a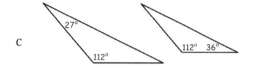

b

c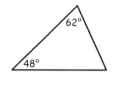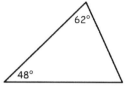

d

22. In $\triangle ABC$, $\overline{DE} \parallel \overline{AC}$.

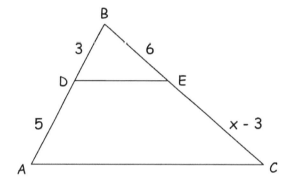

Solve for x.

    a. 8
    b. 10
    c. 11
    d. 13

23. Examine the figure below, in which ΔJKL~ ΔRST.

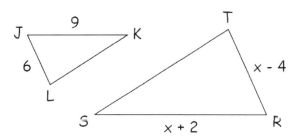

What is the length of $\overline{RS}$?

    a. 10
    b. 12
    c. 16
    d. 18

24. The ratio $\frac{opposite\ leg}{adjacent\ leg}$ represents which trigonometric function?

    a. Sine
    b. Cosine
    c. Tangent
    d. Secant

25. Which of the following pairs of values are equivalent?

    a. sin 17°, cos 73°
    b. sin 58°, cos 58°
    c. sin 64°, sin 26°
    d. sin 145°, sin 35°

26. A building is installing a new ramp at their front entrance.

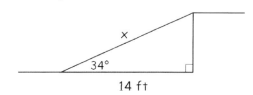

Based on the figure above, what is the length of the ramp, shown by *x*?

    a. 11.6 ft
    b. 16.9 ft
    c. 20.8 ft
    d. 25.0 ft

27. Two hikers start at a ranger station and leave at the same time. One hiker heads due west at 3 miles/hour. The other hiker heads due north at 4 miles/hour. How far apart are the hikers after 2 hours of hiking?

    a. 5 miles
    b. 7 miles
    c. 10 miles
    d. 14 miles

28. The height, h, of the triangle below can also be represented by which of the following expressions?

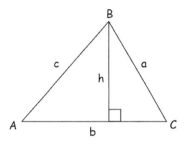

    a. $h = a\cos(C)$
    b. $h = a\sin(C)$
    c. $h = b\cos(C)$
    d. $h = b\sin(C)$

29. Examine the following triangle:

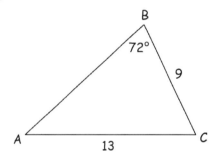

What is the approximate measure of $\angle A$?

    a. 41°
    b. 54°
    c. 67°
    d. 78°

30. While recording the measurements for a plot of land, a surveyor notices a small pond on the property. The surveyor is not able to measure the largest width across the pond directly, but he is able to make the following measurements:

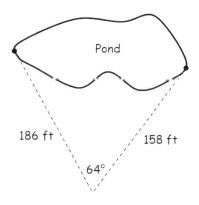

What is the largest distance across the pond?

    a. 82.1 ft
    b. 98.1 ft
    c. 183.8 ft
    d. 244.0 ft

31. Which of the following statements about circles is true?
    a. All circles are similar.
    b. All circles are congruent.
    c. All circles have the same area.
    d. All circles have the same circumference.

32. Based on the figure below, solve for x.

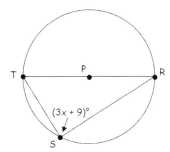

    a. x = 12
    b. x = 17
    c. x = 27
    d. x = 57

33. In Circle O, find the measure of ∠RTS.

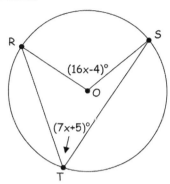

    a. 12°
    b. 26°
    c. 54°
    d. 108°

34. $\overline{AC}$ and $\overline{BC}$ are tangent to the circle. What is the length of $\overline{AC}$?

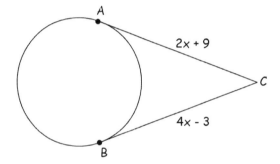

    a. 6
    b. 13
    c. 15
    d. 21

35. Find the length of the arc intercepted by ∠AOB.

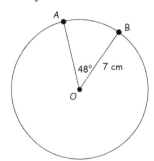

    a. 5.9 cm
    b. 11.7 cm
    c. 20.5 cm
    d. 44.0 cm

36. Find the center and radius of a circle defined by the equation: $x^2 + 2x + y^2 - 8y + 8 = 0$.
    a. $(-1, 4), r = 3$
    b. $(1, -4), r = 9$
    c. $(-2, 8), r = 3$
    d. $(2, -8), r = 9$

37. Find the equation for a parabola with focus $(3, -3)$ and directrix $x = -5$.
    a. $(x + 1)^2 = -20(y + 3)$
    b. $(x + 1)^2 = 16(y + 3)$
    c. $(y + 3)^2 = -20(x - 3)$
    d. $(y + 3)^2 = 16(x + 1)$

38. Given a hyperbola with foci $(5, -4)$ and $(5, 8)$ and a difference of the distances from the foci to a point on the hyperbola of 10, what is the equation of the hyperbola?
    a. $\dfrac{(x-5)^2}{25} + \dfrac{(y-2)^2}{11} = 1$
    b. $\dfrac{(x-5)^2}{25} - \dfrac{(y-2)^2}{11} = 1$
    c. $\dfrac{(y-2)^2}{25} + \dfrac{(x-5)^2}{11} = 1$
    d. $\dfrac{(y-2)^2}{25} - \dfrac{(x-5)^2}{11} = 1$

39. A quadrilateral has the following coordinates $P(-1, 4)$, $Q(5, 2)$, $R(4, -1)$ and $T(-2, 1)$. Quadrilateral $PQRS$ can be best defined as which of the following shapes?
    a. Trapezoid
    b. Square
    c. Rectangle
    d. Parallelogram

40. Which of the following equations represents a line parallel to the line $y = -\dfrac{1}{2}x + 3$ and passes through the point $(-4, -2)$.
    a. $x + 2y = 8$
    b. $x + 2y = -8$
    c. $2x - y = 6$
    d. $2x - y = -6$

41. Examine the number line below.

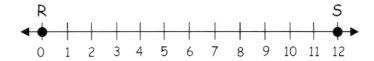

Identify the location of a point T on the number line between R and S such that T is twice as far from S as it is from R.

    a. 4
    b. 6
    c. 8
    d. 10

42. Find the perimeter of ΔABC in the figure below.

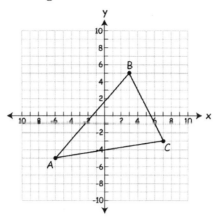

    a. 11.69 units
    b. 21.26 units
    c. 24.14 units
    d. 35.54 units

43. One method for calculating the area of a circle is to dissect it into a number of wedges. The circle below has a radius r and has been evenly dissected into 16 wedges.

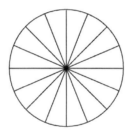

If the wedges are rearranged alternately to create a shape resembling a rectangle, as shown below, what is the approximate length of the rectangle?

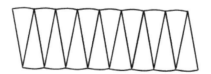

    a. π
    b. πr
    c. r
    d. πr^2

44. While comparing two cones, a student notices that all corresponding cross sections of the cones have the same area. As a result, the student determines that the two cones also have the same volume. The student just discovered which of the following?

    a. Euclid's Principle
    b. Cavalieri's Principle
    c. Dissection Argument
    d. Informal Limit Argument

45. At a sand sculpture festival, one group plans to build a giant sand pyramid on the beach. If the base of the pyramid is to be a square with sides of 10 ft and the pyramid is to be 12 ft tall, how much sand will be needed to build the pyramid?

    a. 260 ft3
    b. 400 ft3
    c. 520 ft3
    d. 1,200 ft^3

46. Kelsey is having a pool party and brought beach balls for the guests to use in the pool. When inflated, each beach ball is 12 inches in diameter. How much air is needed to inflate each beach ball?

    a. 904.8 in^3
    b. 2,714.3 in^3
    c. 7,238.2 in^3
    d. 21,714.7 in^3

47. If the following shape was rotated about the identified axis, what 3-D object will be generated?

Rotation
Axis

    a. Cube
    b. Cylinder
    c. Rectangular Prism
    d. Sphere

48. The shape of Earth can be closely represented by a sphere with a radius of 6,378.1 km. What is the approximate surface area of Earth?

    a. 1.70×108 km^2
    b. 5.11×108 km^2
    c. 1.09×1012 km^2
    d. 3.26×10^{12} km^2

49. A local craft store specializes in selling marbles. To display their most popular sized marble, the store created a 3 ft× 2 ft × 6 in glass box and completely filled the box with 5,184 marbles. What is the density of marbles per cubic foot in the glass box?

    a. 144 marbles/cubic foot
    b. 864 marbles/cubic foot
    c. 1,728 marbles/cubic foot
    d. 15,522 marbles/cubic foot

50. A city has decided to build a fountain in the center of its new park. A 30 ft × 30 ft plot of land will be used for the fountain area. The fountain, which will be circular with a 16 ft diameter, will be centered within that plot of land and the remaining area surrounding the fountain will be covered by a cement walkway. How much land will be covered by the walkway?

    a. 95.8 ft²
    b. 201.1 ft²
    c. 698.9 ft²
    d. 900.0 ft²

Answers and Explanations

Math.Content.G.CO.1

1. B: A circle is defined as the set of all points that are a fixed distance from a given point. In Answer A, an angle is defined as two rays that share a common endpoint. In Answer C, a line segment is defined as all points between and including two given points. In Answer D, a ray is a part of a line starting at a particular point and extending indefinitely in one direction.

Math.Content.G.CO.2

2. A: In Answer A, $\Delta M'N'O'$ is a 180° rotation about the origin of ΔMNO. Therefore, the rotation in Answer A is the transformation that preserves the distance and angle of the original image. Answer B is a dilation of the original image, so it does not preserve distance. Answer C is a horizontal stretch of the original image, so it does not preserve distance or angle. Answer D is a vertical stretching, so it also does not preserve distance or angle.

Math.Content.G.CO.3

3. D: As rectangle $ABCD$ is moved from Quadrant I into Quadrant II, it is rotated in a counterclockwise manner. Therefore, rectangle $ABCD$ can be carried onto its image $A'B'C'D'$ by a 90° counterclockwise rotation about the origin.

Math.Content.G.CO.3

4. A: If a figure is reflected across the line $y = x$, the coordinates of the original figure change from (x, y) to (y, x). In Answer A, the coordinates of image $P'Q'R'S'T'$ are in the order of (y, x) compared to the (x, y) coordinates of $PQRST$, so Answer A shows a reflection across the line $y = x$. Answer B is a reflection across the y-axis. Answer C is a 180° rotation about the origin. Answer D is a reflection across the x-axis.

Math.Content.G.CO.4

5. B: In $\overleftrightarrow{AB}$, A is located at (−6, 2) and B is located at (6, 5). The slope of $\overleftrightarrow{AB} = \frac{5-2}{6-(-6)} = \frac{3}{12} = \frac{1}{4}$. When $\overleftrightarrow{AB}$ is rotated 180° about the origin, the coordinate point for A' becomes (6, −2) and the coordinate point for B' becomes (−6,−5). The slope of $\overleftrightarrow{A'B'} = \frac{-5-(-2)}{-6-6} = \frac{-3}{-12} = \frac{1}{4}$. Since $\overleftrightarrow{AB}$ and $\overleftrightarrow{A'B'}$ have the same slope, the lines are parallel.

Math.Content.G.CO.4

6. A: A translation moves every point of a figure the same distance and in the same direction to create an image. In Answer B, a rotation turns a figure around a central point. In Answer C, a reflection reflects a figure across a given line to create a mirror image. In Answer D, a dilation changes the size of a figure while still maintaining its shape.

Math.Content.G.CO.5

7. B: In the figure, ΔABC was reflected across the y-axis to get $\Delta A'B'C'$. Therefore, the transformation that occurred was a reflection. A dilation would have changed the size of ΔABC while maintaining the shape. A rotation would have rotated ΔABC about a central point. A translation would have moved each point in ΔABC by the same distance and in the same direction.

Math.Content.G.CO.6

8. C: The translation rule $(x, y) \rightarrow (x - 4, y + 2)$ means that 4 is subtracted from each x-coordinate (or each x-coordinate moves 4 units to the left) and 2 is added to each y-coordinate (or each y-coordinate moves up 2 units). $\Delta P'Q'R'$ in Answer C has each x-coordinate move 4 units left and each y-coordinate move 2 units up. Answer D incorrectly took $x - 4$ to mean move 4 units to the right and took $y + 2$ to mean move 2 units down, as would be the case in equations such as $y = a(x - h)^2 + k$. Answer B had the x and y directions reversed on the coordinate grid. Answer A reversed the x and y directions and moved in the opposite directions, as in Answer B.

Math.Content.G.CO.7

9. A: Two triangles are congruent if and only if corresponding pairs of sides and corresponding pairs of angles are congruent. The triangles in Answer A have all three pairs of corresponding sides and all three pairs of corresponding angles marked congruent. In Answer B, the triangles only show three pairs of congruent sides, so there is not enough information to show that the triangles are congruent. Answer C has two pair of corresponding congruent sides and a pair of non-included angles that are congruent which means there is not enough information to show that those triangles are congruent. Answer D has two right triangles with congruent right angles and congruent hypotenuses, but the corresponding legs are not marked as congruent, so there is not enough information to show that those triangles are congruent.

Math.Content.G.CO.8

10. D: For two triangles to be proved congruent by SAS, the triangles need two pairs of corresponding congruent sides and the angle between them also needs to be congruent. In order to include the given congruent angles, the needed pair of congruent sides must be $\overline{BC} \cong \overline{EF}$.

Math.Content.G.CO.8

11. D: In the figure, it shows that $\overline{AC} \cong \overline{DC}$ and $\overline{AB} \cong \overline{DB}$. Although there is no congruent marking on side BC, since the two triangles share that side, it must be that $\overline{BC} \cong \overline{BC}$ by the reflexive property. Therefore, since all three pairs of corresponding sides are congruent, then $\Delta ABC \cong \Delta DBC$ by the SSS triangle congruence.

Math.Content.G.CO.9

12. C: In order to find the measure of $\angle ABC$, we first need to solve for x. In the figure, the angles are vertical angles. According to the Vertical Angle Theorem, vertical angles are congruent. Therefore, to solve for x, we set up an equation as $4x+12 = 5x-3$. After subtracting $4x$ from both sides and adding 3 to both sides, the equation becomes $15 = x$. Next, substitute the value of x into the expression for the measure of $\angle ABC$: $4(15)+12 = 60+12 = 72°$. Answer A is just the value of x. Answer B is the measure of $\angle ABC$ if the angles were incorrectly treated as complementary. Answer D is the measure of $\angle ABC$ if the angles were incorrectly treated as supplementary.

Math.Content.G.CO.9

13. B: The Corresponding Angles Theorem states that if two parallel lines are cut by a transversal, then the pairs of corresponding angles are congruent. Since $\angle 3$ and $\angle 7$ are corresponding and lines p and q are parallel, then $\angle 3 \cong \angle 7$, which means that $m\angle 3 = m\angle 7$. By substitution, that equation becomes $8x + 24 = 10x - 6$. After subtracting $8x$ from both sides and adding 6 to both sides, the

- 112 -

equation simplifies as 30 = 2*x*. Divide both sides by 2 to get 15 = *x*. Substituting for the value of *x*, $m\angle 3 = 8(15) + 24 = 120 + 24 = 144°$. Based on the figure, it is seen that $\angle 3$ and $\angle 4$ are supplementary, so $m\angle 3 + m\angle 4 = 180°$. After substituting for the measure of $\angle 3$, the equation becomes $144° + m\angle 4 = 180°$. Subtract 144 from both sides to get $m\angle 4 = 36°$. Answer A is the value of *x*. Answer C is the $m\angle 4$ if $\angle 3$ and $\angle 7$ were incorrectly set up as supplementary angles. Answer D is the measure of $\angle 3$.

Math.Content.G.CO.10

14. D: According to the Mid-Segment Theorem, the segment joining the midpoints of the two sides of a triangle is half the length of the third side. Therefore, $AE = 2(BD)$, so by substitution, $5x - 5 = 2(2x + 1)$. This equation can be simplified as $5x - 5 = 4x + 2$. After subtracting $4x$ from both sides and adding 5 to both sides, the equation becomes $x = 7$. To find the measure of $\overline{BD}$, substitute for *x* to get $2(7) + 1 = 14 + 1 = 15$. Answer A is the value of *x* if the equation was incorrectly set up as $AE = BD$. Answer B is the measure of $\overline{BD}$ if the equation was incorrectly set up as $AE = BD$. Answer C is just the value of *x*, but the question asks for the measure of $\overline{BD}$.

Math.Content.G.CO.11

15. D: Based on the figure, we can see that $JN + NL = JL$. One of the theorems about parallelograms states that the diagonals of a parallelogram bisect each other. Therefore, according to the figure, $JN = NL$, which means that the equation $JN + NL = JL$ can be rewritten as $JN + JN = JL$. Substituting the expressions for JL and JN, the equation becomes $4x + 7 + 4x + 7 = 13x - 11$. Simplifying the left side of the equation results in $8x + 14 = 13x - 11$. After subtracting $8x$ from both sides and adding 11 to both sides, the equation becomes $25 = 5x$. Divide both sides of the equation by 5 to get $5 = x$. Then, substitute that value for *x* into the expression for JN: $4(5) + 7 = 20 + 7 = 27$. Answer B is just the value of *x*. Answer A is the value for *x* if the equation was incorrectly set up as just $4x + 7 = 13x - 11$. Answer C is the length of $\overline{JN}$ if the equation was incorrectly set up as $4x + 7 = 13x - 11$.

Math.Content.G.CO.12

16. B: "Without changing the compass width, place the compass on the new point, which is not on the segment, and then draw an arc in the area where the other endpoint will be located" is a necessary step when copying a line segment.

Math.Content.G.CO.13

17. C: In order to inscribe a square in a circle, it is necessary to use the endpoints of the diameter as circle centers and draw two intersecting circles. Therefore, Answer C is the step needed to construct a square inscribed in a circle. Answer A is a step in copying a line segment. Answer B is a step in bisecting an angle. Answer D is a step in inscribing an equilateral triangle or a hexagon in a circle.

Math.Content.G.SRT.1a

18. A: The coordinates of points *W* and *Z* are $W(-6, -2)$ and $Z(3, -2)$, which creates a slope for $\overleftrightarrow{WZ} = \frac{-2-(-2)}{3-(-6)} = \frac{0}{9} = 0$. After the dilation by a scale factor of 3, the coordinates of points W' and Z' are $W'(-18, -6)$ and $Z'(9, -6)$, which creates a slope for $\overleftrightarrow{W'Z'} = \frac{-6-(-6)}{9-(-18)} = \frac{0}{27}$. Since $\overleftrightarrow{WZ}$ and $\overleftrightarrow{W'Z'}$ both have a slope of 0, the lines are parallel to each other.

Math.Content.G.SRT.1b

19. C: To determine the scale factor of the dilation, compare the coordinates of $\Delta J'K'L'$ to the coordinates of ΔJKL. J is at $(-2 \ -3)$ and J' is at $(-4, -6)$, which means that the coordinates of J were multiplied by a scale factor of 2 to get the coordinates of J'. K is at $(1, 3)$ and K' is at $(2, 6)$. L is at $(4, -1)$ and L' is at $(8, -2)$. As can be seen, the coordinates of K and L were also multiplied by a scale factor of 2 to get to the coordinates of K' and L'. Answer B is the scale factor going from $\Delta J'K'L'$ to ΔJKL. Answer D results if 3 was incorrectly added or subtracted from the y-coordinates in points K and L to get K' and L'. Answer A is the reciprocal of answer D.

Math.Content.G.SRT.2

20. A: If two triangles are similar, then all pairs of corresponding sides are proportional. In order for ΔRST to be similar to ΔXYZ, we need $\frac{RS}{XY} = \frac{RT}{XZ} = \frac{ST}{YZ}$. Substituting in for those values becomes $\frac{24}{8} = \frac{12}{4} = \frac{30}{YZ}$. Simplifying the fractions results in $\frac{3}{1} = \frac{3}{1} = \frac{30}{YZ}$. Therefore, in order for the triangles to be similar, we need $\frac{3}{1} = \frac{30}{YZ}$. After cross-multiplying the terms, it becomes $3(YZ) = 30(1)$, $3(YZ) = 30$. Divide both sides by 3 to get $YZ = 10$. Answer B saw that 30 was 6 more than 24 and then incorrectly added 6 to 8 to get 14. Answer C incorrectly set up the scale factor as $\frac{24}{8} = \frac{2}{1}$ and set $\frac{2}{1} = \frac{30}{YZ}$ to get $YZ = 15$. Answer D saw that 30 was 18 more than 12 and then incorrectly added 18 to 4 to get 22.

Math.Content.G.SRT.3

21. D: The triangles in Answer D do not have any sides listed and the two corresponding angles that are listed are congruent. Therefore, the triangles in Answer D can be proved similar using the AA Similarity Theorem. In Answer A, the triangles are similar by the SSS Similarity Theorem since all corresponding sides are proportional. In Answer B, the triangles are similar by the SAS similarity theorem since the two pairs of corresponding sides are proportional and the angles between the sides are congruent. In Answer C, the triangles are not similar since the first triangle has angles of 112°, 27° and then 41°, while the second triangle has angles of 112°, 36° and 32°.

Math.Content.G.SRT.4

22. D: One theorem about triangles states that a line parallel to one side of a triangle divides the other two sides proportionally. Since $\overline{DE} \parallel \overline{AC}$, it means that $\frac{BD}{DA} = \frac{BE}{EC}$. Substituting in for those values results in $\frac{3}{5} = \frac{6}{x-3}$. After cross-multiplying, the equation becomes $3(x-3) = (6)(5)$, which simplifies as $3x - 9 = 30$. After adding 9 to both sides, the equation is now $3x = 39$. Divide both sides by 3 to get $x = 13$. Answer A incorrectly results if it is believed that $x - 3$ is equivalent to the 5 on the other side of the triangle. Answer B is the length of $\overline{EC}$, but not the value of x. Answer C incorrectly results if it is believed that since 5 is two more than 3, that $x - 3$ should be two more than 6, such that $x - 3 = 8$.

Math.Content.G.SRT.5

23. D: Since $\Delta JKL \sim \Delta RST$, it means that the sides are proportional. Therefore, $\frac{JL}{RT} = \frac{JK}{RS}$. Substituting for those segments leads to the proportion $\frac{6}{x-4} = \frac{9}{x+2}$. Cross-multiplying results in $6(x+2) = 9(x-4)$. After distributing, the equation becomes $6x + 12 = 9x - 36$. Subtract $6x$ from both sides and add 36 to both sides to get 48 = 3x. Divide both sides by 3 to get 16 = x. Substituting 16 in for x, the length of $\overline{RS}$ = 16 + 2 = 18. In Answer A, 6x + 12 = 9x – 36 was incorrectly simplified with 36 – 12 instead of 12 + 36 to get 24 = 3x and 8 = x, which led to the length of 8 + 2 = 10. Answer B is the length of $\overline{RT}$ instead of $\overline{RS}$. Answer C is the value of x instead of the length of $\overline{RS}$.

Math.Content.G.SRT.6

24. C: The ratio $\frac{opposite\ leg}{adjacent\ leg}$ represents the tangent function. In Answer A, sine is $\frac{opposite\ leg}{hypotenuse}$. In Answer B, cosine is $\frac{adjacent\ leg}{hypotenuse}$. In Answer D, secant is $\frac{hypotenuse}{adjacent\ leg}$.

Math.Content.G.SRT.7

25. A: The sine of one angle is equivalent to the cosine of the complementary angle, that is $\sin a = \cos(90 - a)$. Therefore, in Answer A, 17° and 73° are complementary angles, so sin 17° = cos 73°. Answer B is the cosine of the same angle instead of the complementary angle value. Answer C is the complementary angle, but it is in terms of sine instead of cosine. Answer D uses supplementary angles instead of complementary angles, and they are both sine instead of one being cosine.

Math.Content.G.SRT.8

26. B: Based on the location of the 34°, the 14 ft section is the adjacent leg and the ramp length is the hypotenuse of the right triangle. Therefore, in order to solve for x, it needs to be set up as $\cos 34° = \frac{adjacent\ leg}{hypotenuse}$ or $\cos 34° = \frac{14}{x}$. The value of x is found using the calculation $x = \frac{14}{\cos 34°} = 16.9$ ft. Answer A incorrectly set up the equation as $\cos 34° = \frac{x}{14}$. Answer C incorrectly used $\tan 34° = \frac{14}{x}$. Answer D incorrectly used $\sin 34° = \frac{14}{x}$.

Math.Content.G.SRT.8

27. C: Hiking due west at 3 miles/hour, the first hiker will have gone 6 miles after 2 hours. Hiking due north at 4 miles/hour, the second hiker will have gone 8 miles after 2 hours. Since one hiker headed west and the other headed north, their distance from each other can be drawn as:

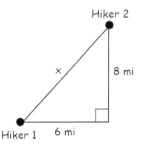

Since the distance between the two hikers is the hypotenuse of a right triangle and we know the lengths of the two legs of the right triangle, the Pythagorean Theorem $(a^2 + b^2 = c^2)$ is used to find the value of x. Therefore, $6^2 + 8^2 = x^2, 36 + 64 = x^2, 100 = x^2, 10 = x$. Answer A is the distance between the hikers after only 1 hour of hiking. Answer B incorrectly added the distances hiked after 1 hour. Answer D incorrectly added the distances hiked after 2 hours.

28. B: In relation to $\angle C$, the height, h, is the opposite leg of the right triangle and side a is the hypotenuse of the right triangle. Therefore, $\sin(C) = \frac{opposite\ leg}{hypotenuse}$, which can be rewritten as $\sin(C) = \frac{h}{a}$. Solving for h results in $h = a\sin(C)$.

29. A: Since the figure shows the measure of $\angle B$, the length of the side opposite of $\angle B$, the length of the side opposite of $\angle A$, and it asks for the measure of $\angle A$, the Law of Sines is needed to find the missing angle measure. The Law of Sines is $\frac{\sin A}{a} = \frac{\sin B}{b} = \frac{\sin C}{c}$, but to solve this problem we only need $\frac{\sin A}{a} = \frac{\sin B}{b}$. By substitution, that equation becomes $\frac{\sin A}{9} = \frac{\sin 72°}{13}$. Solving for A, the equation becomes $A = \sin^{-1}\left(\frac{9\sin 72°}{13}\right) = 41.2°$, which is approximately $41°$. In Answer B, $72°$ was subtracted from $180°$, and the resulting value was divided by 2. Answer C is the measure of $\angle C$. Answer D is the measure of $\angle A$ if the equation was incorrectly set up as $\frac{\cos A}{a} = \frac{\cos B}{b}$.

30. C: Since the surveyor was able to determine the distance from a given spot to the two farthest ends of the pond and determine the measure of the angle between those distance lines, the Law of Cosines can be used to find the largest distance across the pond, which we will call x. Law of Cosines is $c^2 = a^2 + b^2 - 2ab\cos(C)$. If we let $a = 186$, $b = 158$ and $c = x$, then the Law of Cosines becomes $x^2 = 186^2 + 158^2 - 2(186)(158)\cos(64°)$. This simplifies as $x^2 = 33,794.30$. Therefore, $x = 183.8$ ft. Answer A used sine instead of cosine in the formula. Answer B incorrectly used the Pythagorean Theorem as $x^2 + 158^2 = 186^2$. Answer D incorrectly used the Pythagorean Theorem as $158^2 + 186^2 = x^2$.

31. A: Since all circles can be different sizes with different radii, all circles cannot be congruent, have the same area or have the same circumference. However, since all circles maintain the same shape and the ratio Circumference/Diameter is always equal to π, all circles are similar.

32. C: In the figure, the measure of $\angle RST$ is shown to be $(3x + 9)°$. Since $\angle RST$ is inscribed in the semicircle of Circle P, as R and T are endpoints of the diameter, Thale's Theorem tells us $\angle RST$ is a right angle. Therefore, $3x + 9 = 90$. After subtracting 9 from both sides, the equation becomes $3x = 81$. Divide both sides by 3 to get $x = 27$. Answer A set up the equation as $3x + 9 = 45$. Answer B set up the equation as if the triangle were equilateral: $3x + 9 = 60$. Answer D noticed that $\angle RST$ was an inscribed angle that opened up to the semicircle, but then forgot to divide 180 by 2 to get the measure of the angle, so the equation incorrectly used was $3x + 9 = 180$.

33. C: In Circle O, $\angle ROS$ is a central angle and $\angle RTS$ is an inscribed angle. The relationship between those two types of angles is that an inscribed angle is half the measure of a central angle if they share two points on the circle. Therefore, $m\angle ROS = 2(m\angle RTS)$. By substitution, that equation becomes $16x - 4 = 2(7x+5)$. Simplifying that equation results in $16x - 4 = 14x + 10$. After subtracting 14x from both sides and adding 4 to both sides, the equation becomes $2x = 14$. Divide both sides by 2 to get $x = 7$. Substituting that value for x into the expression for $m\angle RTS = 7(7) + 5 = 49 + 5 = 54°$. Answer A is the measure of $\angle RTS$ if the expressions were incorrectly set equal to each other. Answer B is the answer if the equation was correctly simplified to $16x - 4 = 14x + 10$, but then it was incorrectly simplified as $10 - 4$, instead of $10 + 4$, to get $2x = 6$. Answer D is the measure of $\angle ROS$.

Math.Content.G.C.4

34. D: Two segments that are tangent to a circle from the same point outside the circle are congruent. Therefore, $\overline{AC} \cong \overline{BC}$. By substitution, that becomes $2x + 9 = 4x - 3$. After subtracting $2x$ from both sides and adding 3 to both sides, the equation becomes $12 = 2x$. Divide both sides by 2 to get $6 = x$. To find the length of $\overline{AC}$, substitute the value for x to get $2(6) + 9 = 12 + 9 = 21$. Answer A is the value of x. Answer B is the answer if $2x + 9 = 4x - 3$ was incorrectly simplified by adding $2x$ both sides to get $12 = 6x$. Answer C is the answer if $2x + 9 = 4x - 3$ was incorrectly simplified by subtracting 3 from both sides to get $6 = 2x$.

Math.Content.G.C.5

35. A: The length of an arc intercepted by a central angle is calculated using the equation: $\frac{Central\ Angle\ Measure}{360°} \times 2\pi r$. Since the central angle measure is 48° and the radius is 7 cm, the equation becomes: $\frac{48°}{360°} \times 2\pi(7\text{ cm}) = 5.9$ cm. Answer B used the diameter length instead of the radius in the calculation. Answer C is the area of sector AOB. Answer D is the circumference of the circle.

Math.Content.G.GPE.1

36. A: In order to determine the center and radius of the circle, we need to complete the square. Therefore, the equation can first be rewritten as: $x^2 + 2x + y^2 - 8y = -8$. Then, look at the x and y parts separately. For $x^2 + 2x$, we need to add $\left(\frac{2}{2}\right)^2 = (1)^2 = 1$ to both sides of the equation. For $y^2 - 8y$, we need to add $\left(\frac{-8}{2}\right)^2 = (-4)^2 = 16$ to both sides of the equation. Now, $x^2 + 2x + y^2 - 8y = -8$ becomes $x^2 + 2x + 1 + y^2 - 8y + 16 = -8 + 1 + 16$ and simplifies as $(x^2 + 2x + 1) + (y^2 - 8y + 16) = 9$. We can then factor the x and y parts separately to get $(x + 1)^2 + (y - 4)^2 = 9$. Therefore, the center of the circle is as $(-1, 4)$. The radius of the circle is the square root of 9, which is 3. In Answer B, the radius is squared and the center coordinates have the opposite signs. Answers C and D incorrectly factored the equation as $(x + 2)^2 + (y - 8)^2 = 9$, in which C took the center coordinates as $(-2, 8)$ and D took the center coordinates as $(2, -8)$.

Math.Content.G.GPE.2

37. D: Since the focus is at $(3, -3)$ and the directrix is the line $x = -5$, the vertex of the parabola is halfway between those values. Therefore, the vertex is located at $(-1, -3)$. Since the focus is located to the right of the vertex, the parabola opens to the right. A parabola that opens to the right has the general equation of $(y - k)^2 = 4p(x - h)$, where (h, k) is the vertex and the absolute value of p is the distance between the focus and the vertex and the distance between the vertex and directrix. In this problem, the focus is $(3, -3)$ and the vertex is $(-1, -3)$, so $|p| = |3 - (-1)| = |4| = 4$. Since the focus is to the right of the vertex, the value of p is positive, so $p = 4$. Substituting the values for the vertex and p into the equation, it becomes: $(y - (-3))^2 = 4(4)(x - (-1))$, $(y + 3)^2 = 16(x + 1)$. Answer A incorrectly set up the equation as $(x - h)^2 = 4p(y - k)$ and then incorrectly used the

- 117 -

focus for (h, k) and the directrix for p. Answer B incorrectly set up the equation as $(x - h)^2 = 4p(y - k)$. Answer C correctly used the equation of $(y - k)^2 = 4p(x - h)$, but then incorrectly used the focus for (h, k) and the directrix for p.

Math.Content.G.GPE.3

38. D: Since the foci are located along the line $x = 5$, the transverse axis of the hyperbola is vertical. This means the general equation for the hyperbola is $\frac{(y-k)^2}{a^2} - \frac{(x-h)^2}{b^2} = 1$, where (h, k) is the center of the hyperbola, and a is half the difference of the distances from the foci to a point on the hyperbola. Since the center is located between the foci of $(5, -4)$ and $(5, 8)$, the center of the hyperbola is located at $(5, 2)$ and the distance from the center to each focus, c, is 6. The difference of the distances from the foci to a point on the hyperbola is equivalent to $2a$. Therefore, $2a = 10$, so $a = 5$ and $a^2 = 25$. To find the value of b^2, we use the equation $b^2 = c^2 - a^2$. Substituting in for that equation, $b^2 = 6^2 - 5^2 = 36 - 25 = 11$. Based on the center $(5, 2)$, $a^2 = 25$ and $b^2 = 11$, the equation for the hyperbola becomes $\frac{(y-2)^2}{25} - \frac{(x-5)^2}{11} = 1$. Answer C used addition instead of subtraction in the equation. Answers A and B reversed the $(x - 5)$ and $(y - 2)$ values and answer A used addition instead of subtraction.

Math.Content.G.GPE.4

39. C: First, plot the coordinate points to get an idea for the basic shape, as shown below.

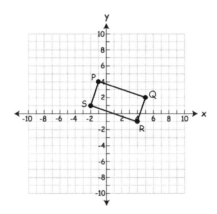

Next, use the distance formula $\left(d = \sqrt{(x_2 - x_1)^2 + (y_2 - y_1)^2}\right)$ to determine the lengths of all four sides: $PQ = \sqrt{(5 - -1)^2 + (2 - 4)^2} = 6.32$, $QR = \sqrt{(4 - 5)^2 + (-1 - 2)^2} = 3.16$, $RS = \sqrt{(-2 - 4)^2 + (1 - -1)^2} = 6.32$, $SP = \sqrt{(-1 - -2)^2 + (4 - 1)^2} = 3.16$. This shows that the lengths of $PQ = RS$ and $QR = PS$. Next calculate the slopes of the four sides: Slope of $\overline{PQ} = \frac{2-4}{5-(-1)} = \frac{-2}{6} = -\frac{1}{3}$, Slope of $\overline{QR} = \frac{-1-2}{4-5} = \frac{-3}{-1} = 3$, Slope of $\overline{RS} = \frac{1-(-1)}{-2-4} = \frac{2}{-6} = -\frac{1}{3}$, Slope of $\overline{SP} = \frac{4-1}{-1-(-2)} = \frac{3}{1} = 3$. Since the slopes of $\overline{PQ}$ and $\overline{QR}$ are opposite reciprocal, it means that those segments are perpendicular and form 90°angles. Similarly, $\overline{QR}$ and $\overline{RS}$, $\overline{RS}$ and $\overline{SP}$, and $\overline{SP}$ and $\overline{PQ}$ all have opposite reciprocal slopes, so those segments are also perpendicular to each other and form 90°angles. Since quadrilateral $PQRS$ has four right angles and the lengths of the opposite sides of the quadrilateral are congruent, this shape is a rectangle.

Math.Content.G.GPE.5

40. B: The slope of the original line is $m = -\frac{1}{2}$. Since the new line needs to be parallel, the new line's slope will be equal to the original slope of $m = -\frac{1}{2}$. The given point is (–4, –2), which is equivalent to (x_1, y_1) in the point-slope equation of $y - y_1 = m(x - x_1)$. Substituting the slope and given point, the point-slope equation becomes $y - (-2) = -\frac{1}{2}(x - (-4))$. Simplifying this equation becomes $y + 2 = -\frac{1}{2}(x + 4)$. Distributing on the right side of the equation results in $y + 2 = -\frac{1}{2}x - 2$. Subtract 2 from both sides of the equation to get the parallel line of $y = -\frac{1}{2}x - 4$. Then, convert the point-slope form into standard form by first adding $\frac{1}{2}x$ to both sides of the equation: $\frac{1}{2}x + y = -4$. Then multiply every term by 2 to cancel out the $\frac{1}{2}$ fraction to get: $x + 2y = -8$. Answer A incorrectly set up the point-slope equation as $y - 2 = -\frac{1}{2}(x - 4)$. Answers C and D used the perpendicular (or opposite reciprocal) slope. Answer C also incorrectly set up the given points in the equation as was done in Answer A.

Math.Content.G.GPE.6

41. A: If point T is twice as far from S as it is from R, it means that the ratio of distance from T to R and S is 1:2, respectively. Therefore, the line segment can be broken up into 1 + 2 = 3 equal segments. The total distance between points R and S is 12 – 0 = 12 units. If we divide 12 by 3, each equal segment is 4 units in length. We then can multiply the ratio by 4 to get the actual distances from T to R and S, 1(4):2(4) = 4:8. So, T is located 4 units from R and 8 units from S. Since R is located at 0, it means that 0 + 4 = 4. Answer B is just halfway between points R and S. Answer C is the point twice as far from R as it is from S. Answer D is a point two units from S instead of twice as far from S than R.

Math.Content.G.GPE.7

42. D: The perimeter of $\triangle ABC$ is $AB + BC + AC$. In order to find the perimeter, we need to find the length of each side of the triangle. To do this, apply the distance formula to the sides AB, BC and AC. The coordinates of the triangle vertices are $A(-6, -5)$, $B(3, 5)$, and $C(7, -3)$. The distance formula is: $d = \sqrt{(x_2 - x_1)^2 + (y_2 - y_1)^2}$. The length of side $AB = \sqrt{(3 - -6)^2 + (5 - -5)^2} = \sqrt{(9)^2 + (10)^2} = \sqrt{81 + 100} = \sqrt{181} = 13.45$. The length of side $BC = \sqrt{(7 - 3)^2 + (-3 - 5)^2} = \sqrt{(4)^2 + (-8)^2} = \sqrt{16 + 64} = \sqrt{80} = 8.94$. The length of side $AC = \sqrt{(7 - -6)^2 + (-3 - -5)^2} = \sqrt{(13)^2 + (2)^2} = \sqrt{169 + 4} = \sqrt{173} = 13.15$. Therefore, the perimeter of $\triangle ABC$ is 13.45 + 8.94 + 13.15 = 35.54 units. Answer A did not square the values after subtracting the pairs of x and y values. Answer B incorrectly set up the distance formula as $d = \sqrt{(x_2 + x_1)^2 + (y_2 + y_1)^2}$. Answer C incorrectly subtracted the smaller squared value from the larger squared value under the radical for each side.

Math.Content.G.GMD.1

43. B: When the wedges are rearranged into the rectangle, half of the wedge arcs form the top length of the rectangle and the other half of the wedge arcs form the bottom length of the rectangle. Since all of the wedge arcs combine to form the entire circumference of the circle, the length of the rectangle is half of the circumference of the circle. The formula for the circumference of a circle with radius r is $C = 2\pi r$. Half of that circumference is $\left(\frac{1}{2}\right) 2\pi r = \pi r$. Answer C is the width of the rectangle. Answer D is the area of the rectangle.

Math.Content.G.GMD.2

44. B: Cavalier's principle states that if all corresponding cross sections of two solids have the same area, then those two solids also have the same volume. Euclid's Principles states that if p is a prime number and p divides ab, then either p divides a or p divides b. The dissection argument involves breaking down a shape or solid into smaller shapes in order to determine the formula of that shape or solid. The informal limit argument deals with finding the area of a circle by having an increasing number of triangles of the same size extend from the center of the circle to the edge of the circle and then determining the area of the circle with an infinite number of triangles on the interior.

Math.Content.G.GMD.3

45. B: The volume of the pyramid is the amount of sand needed to build the pyramid. The formula for the volume of a pyramid is $V = \frac{1}{3}BH$, where B is the area of the base and H is the height of the pyramid. Since the base is a square with sides of 10 ft, the area of the base is 10 ft × 10 ft = 100 ft². The height of the pyramid is 12 ft. Therefore, by substitution, $V = \frac{1}{3}BH$ becomes $V = \frac{1}{3}(100 \text{ ft}^2)(12 \text{ ft}) = 400$ ft³. Answer A is the lateral area of the pyramid. Answer B is lateral area after forgetting to multiply by $\frac{1}{2}$ in the lateral area formula. Answer D used the volume formula of $V = BH$ instead of $V = \frac{1}{3}BH$.

Math.Content.G.GMD.3

46. A: A beach ball is the shape of a sphere and the amount of air needed to inflate each beach ball can be expressed as the volume of the beach ball. The formula for the volume of a sphere is $V = \frac{4}{3}\pi r^3$, where r is the radius of the sphere. Since each beach ball has a diameter of 12 inches, the radius is half of the diameter, or 6 inches. Therefore, by substitution, $V = \frac{4}{3}\pi r^3$ becomes $V = \frac{4}{3}\pi(6 \text{ in})^3 = 904.8$ in³. Answer B forgot to divide by 3. Answer C used the diameter instead of the radius. Answer D forgot to divide by 3 and used the diameter instead of the radius.

Math.Content.G.GMD.4

47. B: When the rectangle is rotated about the shown vertical axis, it will create circular bases along the top and bottom while still maintaining the vertical line along the sides. Therefore, the 3-D object generated will be a cylinder.

Math.Content.G.MG.1

48. B: The formula for the surface area of a sphere is $SA = 4\pi r^2$. Since the radius of Earth is 6,378.1 km, the surface area of the Earth is calculated as $SA = 4\pi(6,378.1 \text{ km})^2 = 5.11 \times 10^8$ km². Answer A incorrectly used the formula $\frac{4}{3}\pi r^2$ for the surface area. Answer C is the volume of Earth. Answer D incorrectly used the formula $4\pi r^3$ for the surface area.

Math.Content.G.MG.2

49. C: To determine the density of marbles per cubic foot, the calculation takes the number of marbles in the box divided by the volume of the box. The dimensions of the box are 3 ft× 2 ft × 6 in. Since the dimensions are not all in the same unit, 6 in is converted into 0.5 ft. The volume of the box then becomes 3 ft × 2 ft × 0.5 ft = 3 ft³. The density of marbles per cubic foot is then calculated as $\frac{5,184\ marbles}{3\ ft^3}$ = 1,728 marbles/cubic foot. Answer A incorrectly calculated the volume of the box by not converting 6 in into feet and multiplied 3 × 2 × 6 to get 36 ft³. Answer B incorrectly divided the number of marbles only by the area of the bottom of the box (3 ft× 2 ft). Answer D incorrectly multiplied the number of marbles by the volume of the box.

Math.Content.G.MG.3

50. C: The amount of land covered by the walkway is the difference between the area of the entire plot of land and the area of the fountain. The area of the entire plot of land is 30 ft × 30 ft = 900 ft². The area of the fountain can be found using the equation $A = \pi r^2$ since the fountain is circular. The diameter of the fountain is 16 ft, so the radius is 8 ft. Therefore, the area of the fountain is $A = \pi(8\ ft)^2$ = 201.1 ft². The area of the walkway is then calculated as 900 ft² – 201.1 ft² = 698.9 ft². Answer A is the area of the walkway if the diameter of the fountain was incorrectly used to calculate the fountain area. Answer B is the area of the fountain. Answer D is the area of the plot of land.

How to Overcome Test Anxiety

Just the thought of taking a test is enough to make most people a little nervous. A test is an important event that can have a long-term impact on your future, so it's important to take it seriously and it's natural to feel anxious about performing well. But just because anxiety is normal, that doesn't mean that it's helpful in test taking, or that you should simply accept it as part of your life. Anxiety can have a variety of effects. These effects can be mild, like making you feel slightly nervous, or severe, like blocking your ability to focus or remember even a simple detail.

If you experience test anxiety—whether severe or mild—it's important to know how to beat it. To discover this, first you need to understand what causes test anxiety.

Causes of Test Anxiety

While we often think of anxiety as an uncontrollable emotional state, it can actually be caused by simple, practical things. One of the most common causes of test anxiety is that a person does not feel adequately prepared for their test. This feeling can be the result of many different issues such as poor study habits or lack of organization, but the most common culprit is time management. Starting to study too late, failing to organize your study time to cover all of the material, or being distracted while you study will mean that you're not well prepared for the test. This may lead to cramming the night before, which will cause you to be physically and mentally exhausted for the test. Poor time management also contributes to feelings of stress, fear, and hopelessness as you realize you are not well prepared but don't know what to do about it.

Other times, test anxiety is not related to your preparation for the test but comes from unresolved fear. This may be a past failure on a test, or poor performance on tests in general. It may come from comparing yourself to others who seem to be performing better or from the stress of living up to expectations. Anxiety may be driven by fears of the future—how failure on this test would affect your educational and career goals. These fears are often completely irrational, but they can still negatively impact your test performance.

> **Review Video:** 3 Reasons You Have Test Anxiety
> Visit mometrix.com/academy and enter code: 428468

Elements of Test Anxiety

As mentioned earlier, test anxiety is considered to be an emotional state, but it has physical and mental components as well. Sometimes you may not even realize that you are suffering from test anxiety until you notice the physical symptoms. These can include trembling hands, rapid heartbeat, sweating, nausea, and tense muscles. Extreme anxiety may lead to fainting or vomiting. Obviously, any of these symptoms can have a negative impact on testing. It is important to recognize them as soon as they begin to occur so that you can address the problem before it damages your performance.

> **Review Video:** 3 Ways to Tell You Have Test Anxiety
> Visit mometrix.com/academy and enter code: 927847

The mental components of test anxiety include trouble focusing and inability to remember learned information. During a test, your mind is on high alert, which can help you recall information and stay focused for an extended period of time. However, anxiety interferes with your mind's natural processes, causing you to blank out, even on the questions you know well. The strain of testing during anxiety makes it difficult to stay focused, especially on a test that may take several hours. Extreme anxiety can take a huge mental toll, making it difficult not only to recall test information but even to understand the test questions or pull your thoughts together.

> **Review Video:** How Test Anxiety Affects Memory
> Visit mometrix.com/academy and enter code: 609003

Effects of Test Anxiety

Test anxiety is like a disease—if left untreated, it will get progressively worse. Anxiety leads to poor performance, and this reinforces the feelings of fear and failure, which in turn lead to poor performances on subsequent tests. It can grow from a mild nervousness to a crippling condition. If allowed to progress, test anxiety can have a big impact on your schooling, and consequently on your future.

Test anxiety can spread to other parts of your life. Anxiety on tests can become anxiety in any stressful situation, and blanking on a test can turn into panicking in a job situation. But fortunately, you don't have to let anxiety rule your testing and determine your grades. There are a number of relatively simple steps you can take to move past anxiety and function normally on a test and in the rest of life.

> **Review Video:** How Test Anxiety Impacts Your Grades
> Visit mometrix.com/academy and enter code: 939819

Physical Steps for Beating Test Anxiety

While test anxiety is a serious problem, the good news is that it can be overcome. It doesn't have to control your ability to think and remember information. While it may take time, you can begin taking steps today to beat anxiety.

Just as your first hint that you may be struggling with anxiety comes from the physical symptoms, the first step to treating it is also physical. Rest is crucial for having a clear, strong mind. If you are tired, it is much easier to give in to anxiety. But if you establish good sleep habits, your body and mind will be ready to perform optimally, without the strain of exhaustion. Additionally, sleeping well helps you to retain information better, so you're more likely to recall the answers when you see the test questions.

Getting good sleep means more than going to bed on time. It's important to allow your brain time to relax. Take study breaks from time to time so it doesn't get overworked, and don't study right before bed. Take time to rest your mind before trying to rest your body, or you may find it difficult to fall asleep.

> **Review Video: The Importance of Sleep for Your Brain**
> Visit mometrix.com/academy and enter code: 319338

Along with sleep, other aspects of physical health are important in preparing for a test. Good nutrition is vital for good brain function. Sugary foods and drinks may give a burst of energy but this burst is followed by a crash, both physically and emotionally. Instead, fuel your body with protein and vitamin-rich foods.

Also, drink plenty of water. Dehydration can lead to headaches and exhaustion, especially if your brain is already under stress from the rigors of the test. Particularly if your test is a long one, drink water during the breaks. And if possible, take an energy-boosting snack to eat between sections.

> **Review Video: How Diet Can Affect your Mood**
> Visit mometrix.com/academy and enter code: 624317

Along with sleep and diet, a third important part of physical health is exercise. Maintaining a steady workout schedule is helpful, but even taking 5-minute study breaks to walk can help get your blood pumping faster and clear your head. Exercise also releases endorphins, which contribute to a positive feeling and can help combat test anxiety.

When you nurture your physical health, you are also contributing to your mental health. If your body is healthy, your mind is much more likely to be healthy as well. So take time to rest, nourish your body with healthy food and water, and get moving as much as possible. Taking these physical steps will make you stronger and more able to take the mental steps necessary to overcome test anxiety.

> **Review Video: How to Stay Healthy and Prevent Test Anxiety**
> Visit mometrix.com/academy and enter code: 877894

Mental Steps for Beating Test Anxiety

Working on the mental side of test anxiety can be more challenging, but as with the physical side, there are clear steps you can take to overcome it. As mentioned earlier, test anxiety often stems from lack of preparation, so the obvious solution is to prepare for the test. Effective studying may be the most important weapon you have for beating test anxiety, but you can and should employ several other mental tools to combat fear.

First, boost your confidence by reminding yourself of past success—tests or projects that you aced. If you're putting as much effort into preparing for this test as you did for those, there's no reason you should expect to fail here. Work hard to prepare; then trust your preparation.

Second, surround yourself with encouraging people. It can be helpful to find a study group, but be sure that the people you're around will encourage a positive attitude. If you spend time with others who are anxious or cynical, this will only contribute to your own anxiety. Look for others who are motivated to study hard from a desire to succeed, not from a fear of failure.

Third, reward yourself. A test is physically and mentally tiring, even without anxiety, and it can be helpful to have something to look forward to. Plan an activity following the test, regardless of the outcome, such as going to a movie or getting ice cream.

When you are taking the test, if you find yourself beginning to feel anxious, remind yourself that you know the material. Visualize successfully completing the test. Then take a few deep, relaxing breaths and return to it. Work through the questions carefully but with confidence, knowing that you are capable of succeeding.

Developing a healthy mental approach to test taking will also aid in other areas of life. Test anxiety affects more than just the actual test—it can be damaging to your mental health and even contribute to depression. It's important to beat test anxiety before it becomes a problem for more than testing.

> **Review Video: Test Anxiety and Depression**
> Visit mometrix.com/academy and enter code: 904704

Study Strategy

Being prepared for the test is necessary to combat anxiety, but what does being prepared look like? You may study for hours on end and still not feel prepared. What you need is a strategy for test prep. The next few pages outline our recommended steps to help you plan out and conquer the challenge of preparation.

Step 1: Scope Out the Test

Learn everything you can about the format (multiple choice, essay, etc.) and what will be on the test. Gather any study materials, course outlines, or sample exams that may be available. Not only will this help you to prepare, but knowing what to expect can help to alleviate test anxiety.

Step 2: Map Out the Material

Look through the textbook or study guide and make note of how many chapters or sections it has. Then divide these over the time you have. For example, if a book has 15 chapters and you have five days to study, you need to cover three chapters each day. Even better, if you have the time, leave an extra day at the end for overall review after you have gone through the material in depth.

If time is limited, you may need to prioritize the material. Look through it and make note of which sections you think you already have a good grasp on, and which need review. While you are studying, skim quickly through the familiar sections and take more time on the challenging parts. Write out your plan so you don't get lost as you go. Having a written plan also helps you feel more in control of the study, so anxiety is less likely to arise from feeling overwhelmed at the amount to cover.

Step 3: Gather Your Tools

Decide what study method works best for you. Do you prefer to highlight in the book as you study and then go back over the highlighted portions? Or do you type out notes of the important information? Or is it helpful to make flashcards that you can carry with you? Assemble the pens, index cards, highlighters, post-it notes, and any other materials you may need so you won't be distracted by getting up to find things while you study.

If you're having a hard time retaining the information or organizing your notes, experiment with different methods. For example, try color-coding by subject with colored pens, highlighters, or post-it notes. If you learn better by hearing, try recording yourself reading your notes so you can listen while in the car, working out, or simply sitting at your desk. Ask a friend to quiz you from your flashcards, or try teaching someone the material to solidify it in your mind.

Step 4: Create Your Environment

It's important to avoid distractions while you study. This includes both the obvious distractions like visitors and the subtle distractions like an uncomfortable chair (or a too-comfortable couch that makes you want to fall asleep). Set up the best study environment possible: good lighting and a comfortable work area. If background music helps you focus, you may want to turn it on, but otherwise keep the room quiet. If you are using a computer to take notes, be sure you don't have any other windows open, especially applications like social media, games, or anything else that could distract you. Silence your phone and turn off notifications. Be sure to keep water close by so you stay hydrated while you study (but avoid unhealthy drinks and snacks).

Also, take into account the best time of day to study. Are you freshest first thing in the morning? Try to set aside some time then to work through the material. Is your mind clearer in the afternoon or evening? Schedule your study session then. Another method is to study at the same time of day that you will take the test, so that your brain gets used to working on the material at that time and will be ready to focus at test time.

Step 5: Study!

Once you have done all the study preparation, it's time to settle into the actual studying. Sit down, take a few moments to settle your mind so you can focus, and begin to follow your study plan. Don't give in to distractions or let yourself procrastinate. This is your time to prepare so you'll be ready to fearlessly approach the test. Make the most of the time and stay focused.

Of course, you don't want to burn out. If you study too long you may find that you're not retaining the information very well. Take regular study breaks. For example, taking five minutes out of every hour to walk briskly, breathing deeply and swinging your arms, can help your mind stay fresh.

As you get to the end of each chapter or section, it's a good idea to do a quick review. Remind yourself of what you learned and work on any difficult parts. When you feel that you've mastered the material, move on to the next part. At the end of your study session, briefly skim through your notes again.

But while review is helpful, cramming last minute is NOT. If at all possible, work ahead so that you won't need to fit all your study into the last day. Cramming overloads your brain with more information than it can process and retain, and your tired mind may struggle to recall even previously learned information when it is overwhelmed with last-minute study. Also, the urgent nature of cramming and the stress placed on your brain contribute to anxiety. You'll be more likely to go to the test feeling unprepared and having trouble thinking clearly.

So don't cram, and don't stay up late before the test, even just to review your notes at a leisurely pace. Your brain needs rest more than it needs to go over the information again. In fact, plan to finish your studies by noon or early afternoon the day before the test. Give your brain the rest of the day to relax or focus on other things, and get a good night's sleep. Then you will be fresh for the test and better able to recall what you've studied.

Step 6: Take a practice test

Many courses offer sample tests, either online or in the study materials. This is an excellent resource to check whether you have mastered the material, as well as to prepare for the test format and environment.

Check the test format ahead of time: the number of questions, the type (multiple choice, free response, etc.), and the time limit. Then create a plan for working through them. For example, if you have 30 minutes to take a 60-question test, your limit is 30 seconds per question. Spend less time on the questions you know well so that you can take more time on the difficult ones.

If you have time to take several practice tests, take the first one open book, with no time limit. Work through the questions at your own pace and make sure you fully understand them. Gradually work up to taking a test under test conditions: sit at a desk with all study materials put away and set a timer. Pace yourself to make sure you finish the test with time to spare and go back to check your answers if you have time.

After each test, check your answers. On the questions you missed, be sure you understand why you missed them. Did you misread the question (tests can use tricky wording)? Did you forget the information? Or was it something you hadn't learned? Go back and study any shaky areas that the practice tests reveal.

Taking these tests not only helps with your grade, but also aids in combating test anxiety. If you're already used to the test conditions, you're less likely to worry about it, and working through tests until you're scoring well gives you a confidence boost. Go through the practice tests until you feel comfortable, and then you can go into the test knowing that you're ready for it.

Test Tips

On test day, you should be confident, knowing that you've prepared well and are ready to answer the questions. But aside from preparation, there are several test day strategies you can employ to maximize your performance.

First, as stated before, get a good night's sleep the night before the test (and for several nights before that, if possible). Go into the test with a fresh, alert mind rather than staying up late to study.

Try not to change too much about your normal routine on the day of the test. It's important to eat a nutritious breakfast, but if you normally don't eat breakfast at all, consider eating just a protein bar. If you're a coffee drinker, go ahead and have your normal coffee. Just make sure you time it so that the caffeine doesn't wear off right in the middle of your test. Avoid sugary beverages, and drink enough water to stay hydrated but not so much that you need a restroom break 10 minutes into the test. If your test isn't first thing in the morning, consider going for a walk or doing a light workout before the test to get your blood flowing.

Allow yourself enough time to get ready, and leave for the test with plenty of time to spare so you won't have the anxiety of scrambling to arrive in time. Another reason to be early is to select a good seat. It's helpful to sit away from doors and windows, which can be distracting. Find a good seat, get out your supplies, and settle your mind before the test begins.

When the test begins, start by going over the instructions carefully, even if you already know what to expect. Make sure you avoid any careless mistakes by following the directions.

Then begin working through the questions, pacing yourself as you've practiced. If you're not sure on an answer, don't spend too much time on it, and don't let it shake your confidence. Either skip it and come back later, or eliminate as many wrong answers as possible and guess among the remaining ones. Don't dwell on these questions as you continue—put them out of your mind and focus on what lies ahead.

Be sure to read all of the answer choices, even if you're sure the first one is the right answer. Sometimes you'll find a better one if you keep reading. But don't second-guess yourself if you do immediately know the answer. Your gut instinct is usually right. Don't let test anxiety rob you of the information you know.

If you have time at the end of the test (and if the test format allows), go back and review your answers. Be cautious about changing any, since your first instinct tends to be correct, but make sure you didn't misread any of the questions or accidentally mark the wrong answer choice. Look over any you skipped and make an educated guess.

At the end, leave the test feeling confident. You've done your best, so don't waste time worrying about your performance or wishing you could change anything. Instead, celebrate the successful completion of this test. And finally, use this test to learn how to deal with anxiety even better next time.

Review Video: 5 Tips to Beat Test Anxiety Visit mometrix.com/academy and enter code: 570656

Important Qualification

Not all anxiety is created equal. If your test anxiety is causing major issues in your life beyond the classroom or testing center, or if you are experiencing troubling physical symptoms related to your anxiety, it may be a sign of a serious physiological or psychological condition. If this sounds like your situation, we strongly encourage you to seek professional help.

How to Overcome Your Fear of Math

The word *math* is enough to strike fear into most hearts. How many of us have memories of sitting through confusing lectures, wrestling over mind-numbing homework, or taking tests that still seem incomprehensible even after hours of study? Years after graduation, many still shudder at these memories.

The fact is, math is not just a classroom subject. It has real-world implications that you face every day, whether you realize it or not. This may be balancing your monthly budget, deciding how many supplies to buy for a project, or simply splitting a meal check with friends. The idea of daily confrontations with math can be so paralyzing that some develop a condition known as *math anxiety*.

But you do NOT need to be paralyzed by this anxiety! In fact, while you may have thought all your life that you're not good at math, or that your brain isn't wired to understand it, the truth is that you may have been conditioned to think this way. From your earliest school days, the way you were taught affected the way you viewed different subjects. And the way math has been taught has changed.

Several decades ago, there was a shift in American math classrooms. The focus changed from traditional problem-solving to a conceptual view of topics, de-emphasizing the importance of learning the basics and building on them. The solid foundation necessary for math progression and confidence was undermined. Math became more of a vague concept than a concrete idea. Today, it is common to think of math, not as a straightforward system, but as a mysterious, complicated method that can't be fully understood unless you're a genius.

This is why you may still have nightmares about being called on to answer a difficult problem in front of the class. Math anxiety is a very real, though unnecessary, fear.

Math anxiety may begin with a single class period. Let's say you missed a day in 6th grade math and never quite understood the concept that was taught while you were gone. Since math is cumulative, with each new concept building on past ones, this could very well affect the rest of your math career. Without that one day's knowledge, it will be difficult to understand any other concepts that link to it. Rather than realizing that you're just missing one key piece, you may begin to believe that you're simply not capable of understanding math.

This belief can change the way you approach other classes, career options, and everyday life experiences, if you become anxious at the thought that math might be required. A student who loves science may choose a different path of study upon realizing that multiple math classes will be required for a degree. An aspiring medical student may hesitate at the thought of going through the necessary math classes. For some this anxiety escalates into a more extreme state known as *math phobia*.

Math anxiety is challenging to address because it is rooted deeply and may come from a variety of causes: an embarrassing moment in class, a teacher who did not explain concepts well and contributed to a shaky foundation, or a failed test that contributed to the belief of math failure.

These causes add up over time, encouraged by society's popular view that math is hard and unpleasant. Eventually a person comes to firmly believe that he or she is simply bad at math. This belief makes it difficult to grasp new concepts or even remember old ones. Homework and test grades begin to slip, which only confirms the belief. The poor performance is not due to lack of ability but is caused by math anxiety.

Math anxiety is an emotional issue, not a lack of intelligence. But when it becomes deeply rooted, it can become more than just an emotional problem. Physical symptoms appear. Blood pressure may rise and heartbeat may quicken at the sight of a math problem – or even the thought of math! This fear leads to a mental block. When someone with math anxiety is asked to perform a calculation, even a basic problem can seem overwhelming and impossible. The emotional and physical response to the thought of math prevents the brain from working through it logically.

The more this happens, the more a person's confidence drops, and the more math anxiety is generated. This vicious cycle must be broken!

The first step in breaking the cycle is to go back to very beginning and make sure you really understand the basics of how math works and why it works. It is not enough to memorize rules for multiplication and division. If you don't know WHY these rules work, your foundation will be shaky and you will be at risk of developing a phobia. Understanding mathematical concepts not only promotes confidence and security, but allows you to build on this understanding for new concepts. Additionally, you can solve unfamiliar problems using familiar concepts and processes.

Why is it that students in other countries regularly outperform American students in math? The answer likely boils down to a couple of things: the foundation of mathematical conceptual understanding and societal perception. While students in the US are not expected to *like* or *get* math, in many other nations, students are expected not only to understand math but also to excel at it.

Changing the American view of math that leads to math anxiety is a monumental task. It requires changing the training of teachers nationwide, from kindergarten through high school, so that they learn to teach the *why* behind math and to combat the wrong math views that students may develop. It also involves changing the stigma associated with math, so that it is no longer viewed as unpleasant and incomprehensible. While these are necessary changes, they are challenging and will take time. But in the meantime, math anxiety is not irreversible—it can be faced and defeated, one person at a time.

False Beliefs

One reason math anxiety has taken such hold is that several false beliefs have been created and shared until they became widely accepted. Some of these unhelpful beliefs include the following:

There is only one way to solve a math problem. In the same way that you can choose from different driving routes and still arrive at the same house, you can solve a math problem using different methods and still find the correct answer. A person who understands the reasoning behind math calculations may be able to look at an unfamiliar concept and find the right answer, just by applying logic to the knowledge they already have. This approach may be different than what is taught in the classroom, but it is still valid. Unfortunately, even many teachers view math as a subject where the best course of action is to memorize the rule or process for each problem rather than as a place for students to exercise logic and creativity in finding a solution.

Many people don't have a mind for math. A person who has struggled due to poor teaching or math anxiety may falsely believe that he or she doesn't have the mental capacity to grasp mathematical concepts. Most of the time, this is false. Many people find that when they are relieved of their math anxiety, they have more than enough brainpower to understand math.

- 131 -

Men are naturally better at math than women. Even though research has shown this to be false, many young women still avoid math careers and classes because of their belief that their math abilities are inferior. Many girls have come to believe that math is a male skill and have given up trying to understand or enjoy it.

Counting aids are bad. Something like counting on your fingers or drawing out a problem to visualize it may be frowned on as childish or a crutch, but these devices can help you get a tangible understanding of a problem or a concept.

Sadly, many students buy into these ideologies at an early age. A young girl who enjoys math class may be conditioned to think that she doesn't actually have the brain for it because math is for boys, and may turn her energies to other pursuits, permanently closing the door on a wide range of opportunities. A child who finds the right answer but doesn't follow the teacher's method may believe that he is doing it wrong and isn't good at math. A student who never had a problem with math before may have a poor teacher and become confused, yet believe that the problem is because she doesn't have a mathematical mind.

Students who have bought into these erroneous beliefs quickly begin to add their own anxieties, adapting them to their own personal situations:

I'll never use this in real life. A huge number of people wrongly believe that math is irrelevant outside the classroom. By adopting this mindset, they are handicapping themselves for a life in a mathematical world, as well as limiting their career choices. When they are inevitably faced with real-world math, they are conditioning themselves to respond with anxiety.

I'm not quick enough. While timed tests and quizzes, or even simply comparing yourself with other students in the class, can lead to this belief, speed is not an indicator of skill level. A person can work very slowly yet understand at a deep level.

If I can understand it, it's too easy. People with a low view of their own abilities tend to think that if they are able to grasp a concept, it must be simple. They cannot accept the idea that they are capable of understanding math. This belief will make it harder to learn, no matter how intelligent they are.

I just can't learn this. An overwhelming number of people think this, from young children to adults, and much of the time it is simply not true. But this mindset can turn into a self-fulfilling prophecy that keeps you from exercising and growing your math ability.

The good news is, each of these myths can be debunked. For most people, they are based on emotion and psychology, NOT on actual ability! It will take time, effort, and the desire to change, but change is possible. Even if you have spent years thinking that you don't have the capability to understand math, it is not too late to uncover your true ability and find relief from the anxiety that surrounds math.

Math Strategies

It is important to have a plan of attack to combat math anxiety. There are many useful strategies for pinpointing the fears or myths and eradicating them:

Go back to the basics. For most people, math anxiety stems from a poor foundation. You may think that you have a complete understanding of addition and subtraction, or even decimals and percentages, but make absolutely sure. Learning math is different from learning other subjects. For example, when you learn history, you study various time periods and places and events. It may be important to memorize dates or find out about the lives of famous people. When you move from US history to world history, there will be some overlap, but a large amount of the information will be new. Mathematical concepts, on the other hand, are very closely linked and highly dependent on each other. It's like climbing a ladder – if a rung is missing from your understanding, it may be difficult or impossible for you to climb any higher, no matter how hard you try. So go back and make sure your math foundation is strong. This may mean taking a remedial math course, going to a tutor to work through the shaky concepts, or just going through your old homework to make sure you really understand it.

Speak the language. Math has a large vocabulary of terms and phrases unique to working problems. Sometimes these are completely new terms, and sometimes they are common words, but are used differently in a math setting. If you can't speak the language, it will be very difficult to get a thorough understanding of the concepts. It's common for students to think that they don't understand math when they simply don't understand the vocabulary. The good news is that this is fairly easy to fix. Brushing up on any terms you aren't quite sure of can help bring the rest of the concepts into focus.

Check your anxiety level. When you think about math, do you feel nervous or uncomfortable? Do you struggle with feelings of inadequacy, even on concepts that you know you've already learned? It's important to understand your specific math anxieties, and what triggers them. When you catch yourself falling back on a false belief, mentally replace it with the truth. Don't let yourself believe that you can't learn, or that struggling with a concept means you'll never understand it. Instead, remind yourself of how much you've already learned and dwell on that past success. Visualize grasping the new concept, linking it to your old knowledge, and moving on to the next challenge. Also, learn how to manage anxiety when it arises. There are many techniques for coping with the irrational fears that rise to the surface when you enter the math classroom. This may include controlled breathing, replacing negative thoughts with positive ones, or visualizing success. Anxiety interferes with your ability to concentrate and absorb information, which in turn contributes to greater anxiety. If you can learn how to regain control of your thinking, you will be better able to pay attention, make progress, and succeed!

Don't go it alone. Like any deeply ingrained belief, math anxiety is not easy to eradicate. And there is no need for you to wrestle through it on your own. It will take time, and many people find that speaking with a counselor or psychiatrist helps. They can help you develop strategies for responding to anxiety and overcoming old ideas. Additionally, it can be very helpful to take a short course or seek out a math tutor to help you find and fix the missing rungs on your ladder and make sure that you're ready to progress to the next level. You can also find a number of math aids online: courses that will teach you mental devices for figuring out problems, how to get the most out of your math classes, etc.

Check your math attitude. No matter how much you want to learn and overcome your anxiety, you'll have trouble if you still have a negative attitude toward math. If you think it's too hard, or just have general feelings of dread about math, it will be hard to learn and to break through the anxiety. Work on cultivating a positive math attitude. Remind yourself that math is not just a hurdle to be cleared, but a valuable asset. When you view math with a positive attitude, you'll be much more likely to understand and even enjoy it. This is something you must do for yourself. You may find it helpful to visit with a counselor. Your tutor, friends, and family may cheer you on in your endeavors. But your greatest asset is yourself. You are inside your own mind – tell yourself what you need to hear. Relive past victories. Remind yourself that you are capable of understanding math. Root out any false beliefs that linger and replace them with positive truths. Even if it doesn't feel true at first, it will begin to affect your thinking and pave the way for a positive, anxiety-free mindset.

Aside from these general strategies, there are a number of specific practical things you can do to begin your journey toward overcoming math anxiety. Something as simple as learning a new note-taking strategy can change the way you approach math and give you more confidence and understanding. New study techniques can also make a huge difference.

Math anxiety leads to bad habits. If it causes you to be afraid of answering a question in class, you may gravitate toward the back row. You may be embarrassed to ask for help. And you may procrastinate on assignments, which leads to rushing through them at the last moment when it's too late to get a better understanding. It's important to identify your negative behaviors and replace them with positive ones:

Prepare ahead of time. Read the lesson before you go to class. Being exposed to the topics that will be covered in class ahead of time, even if you don't understand them perfectly, is extremely helpful in increasing what you retain from the lecture. Do your homework and, if you're still shaky, go over some extra problems. The key to a solid understanding of math is practice.

Sit front and center. When you can easily see and hear, you'll understand more, and you'll avoid the distractions of other students if no one is in front of you. Plus, you're more likely to be sitting with students who are positive and engaged, rather than others with math anxiety. Let their positive math attitude rub off on you.

Ask questions in class and out. If you don't understand something, just ask. If you need a more in-depth explanation, the teacher may need to work with you outside of class, but often it's a simple concept you don't quite understand, and a single question may clear it up. If you wait, you may not be able to follow the rest of the day's lesson. For extra help, most professors have office hours outside of class when you can go over concepts one-on-one to clear up any uncertainties. Additionally, there may be a *math lab* or study session you can attend for homework help. Take advantage of this.

Review. Even if you feel that you've fully mastered a concept, review it periodically to reinforce it. Going over an old lesson has several benefits: solidifying your understanding, giving you a confidence boost, and even giving some new insights into material that you're currently learning! Don't let yourself get rusty. That can lead to problems with learning later concepts.

Teaching Tips

While the math student's mindset is the most crucial to overcoming math anxiety, it is also important for others to adjust their math attitudes. Teachers and parents have an enormous influence on how students relate to math. They can either contribute to math confidence or math anxiety.

As a parent or teacher, it is very important to convey a positive math attitude. Retelling horror stories of your own bad experience with math will contribute to a new generation of math anxiety. Even if you don't share your experiences, others will be able to sense your fears and may begin to believe them.

Even a careless comment can have a big impact, so watch for phrases like *He's not good at math* or *I never liked math*. You are a crucial role model, and your children or students will unconsciously adopt your mindset. Give them a positive example to follow. Rather than teaching them to fear the math world before they even know it, teach them about all its potential and excitement.

Work to present math as an integral, beautiful, and understandable part of life. Encourage creativity in solving problems. Watch for false beliefs and dispel them. Cross the lines between subjects: integrate history, English, and music with math. Show students how math is used every day, and how the entire world is based on mathematical principles, from the pull of gravity to the shape of seashells. Instead of letting students see math as a necessary evil, direct them to view it as an imaginative, beautiful art form – an art form that they are capable of mastering and using.

Don't give too narrow a view of math. It is more than just numbers. Yes, working problems and learning formulas is a large part of classroom math. But don't let the teaching stop there. Teach students about the everyday implications of math. Show them how nature works according to the laws of mathematics, and take them outside to make discoveries of their own. Expose them to math-related careers by inviting visiting speakers, asking students to do research and presentations, and learning students' interests and aptitudes on a personal level.

Demonstrate the importance of math. Many people see math as nothing more than a required stepping stone to their degree, a nuisance with no real usefulness. Teach students that algebra is used every day in managing their bank accounts, in following recipes, and in scheduling the day's events. Show them how learning to do geometric proofs helps them to develop logical thinking, an invaluable life skill. Let them see that math surrounds them and is integrally linked to their daily lives: that weather predictions are based on math, that math was used to design cars and other machines, etc. Most of all, give them the tools to use math to enrich their lives.

Make math as tangible as possible. Use visual aids and objects that can be touched. It is much easier to grasp a concept when you can hold it in your hands and manipulate it, rather than just listening to the lecture. Encourage math outside of the classroom. The real world is full of measuring, counting, and calculating, so let students participate in this. Keep your eyes open for numbers and patterns to discuss. Talk about how scores are calculated in sports games and how far apart plants are placed in a garden row for maximum growth. Build the mindset that math is a normal and interesting part of daily life.

Finally, find math resources that help to build a positive math attitude. There are a number of books that show math as fascinating and exciting while teaching important concepts, for example: *The Math Curse; A Wrinkle in Time; The Phantom Tollbooth;* and *Fractals, Googols and Other Mathematical Tales*. You can also find a number of online resources: math puzzles and games, videos that show math in nature, and communities of math enthusiasts. On a local level, students can compete in a variety of math competitions with other schools or join a math club.

The student who experiences math as exciting and interesting is unlikely to suffer from math anxiety. Going through life without this handicap is an immense advantage and opens many doors that others have closed through their fear.

Self-Check

Whether you suffer from math anxiety or not, chances are that you have been exposed to some of the false beliefs mentioned above. Now is the time to check yourself for any errors you may have accepted. Do you think you're not wired for math? Or that you don't need to understand it since you're not planning on a math career? Do you think math is just too difficult for the average person?

Find the errors you've taken to heart and replace them with positive thinking. Are you capable of learning math? Yes! Can you control your anxiety? Yes! These errors will resurface from time to time, so be watchful. Don't let others with math anxiety influence you or sway your confidence. If you're having trouble with a concept, find help. Don't let it discourage you!

Create a plan of attack for defeating math anxiety and sharpening your skills. Do some research and decide if it would help you to take a class, get a tutor, or find some online resources to fine-tune your knowledge. Make the effort to get good nutrition, hydration, and sleep so that you are operating at full capacity. Remind yourself daily that you are skilled and that anxiety does not control you. Your mind is capable of so much more than you know. Give it the tools it needs to grow and thrive.

Thank You

We at Mometrix would like to extend our heartfelt thanks to you, our friend and patron, for allowing us to play a part in your journey. It is a privilege to serve people from all walks of life who are unified in their commitment to building the best future they can for themselves.

The preparation you devote to these important testing milestones may be the most valuable educational opportunity you have for making a real difference in your life. We encourage you to put your heart into it—that feeling of succeeding, overcoming, and yes, conquering will be well worth the hours you've invested.

We want to hear your story, your struggles and your successes, and if you see any opportunities for us to improve our materials so we can help others even more effectively in the future, please share that with us as well. **The team at Mometrix would be absolutely thrilled to hear from you!** So please, send us an email (support@mometrix.com) and let's stay in touch.

If you'd like some additional help, check out these other resources we offer for your exam:

http://MometrixFlashcards.com/PARCC

Additional Bonus Material

Due to our efforts to try to keep this book to a manageable length, we've created a link that will give you access to all of your additional bonus material.

Please visit http://www.mometrix.com/bonus948/parcchsgeom to access the information.